Habit to read without knowing all the words

단어를 몰라도 읽어내는 습관

WRITTEN BY Stephan Kim, Mr. Sun

- TOEIC시험이 가장 원하는 능력은 무엇일까?
- 문장의 구조를 파악하면 모르는 단어의 의미가 보인다.
- 영어의 기본기가 고득점을 위한 가장 쉬운 방법!

단어를 몰라도
읽어내는
습관

1판1쇄 2013년 12월 15일

저   자 Stephan Kim & Mr. Sun
펴 낸 곳 OLD STAIRS
출판 등록 2008년1월10일 제313-2010-284호
주   소 서울시 마포구 동교로 18길 9-7
이 메 일 oldstairs@daum.net

가격 13,000원
ISBN 978-89-97221-20-2
     978-89-97221-19-6 (세트)

이 책의 내용의 일부 또는 전부를 재사용하시려면 반드시 OLD STAIRS의 동의를 얻어야 합니다.
잘못 만들어진 책은 구입하신 서점에서 교환해 드립니다.

Habit to read without knowing all the words

단어를 몰라도 읽어내는 습관

토익시험이 가장 원하는 능력은 무엇일까?

토익은 그 이름이 의미하듯이 커뮤니케이션 능력을 수치화하는 시험입니다. 그러기 위해서 파트1부터 7까지 다양한 형식의 시험을 치르게 됩니다. 이를 통해 읽기, 쓰기, 듣기, 말하기에 필요한 요소를 골고루 파악할 수 있도록 디자인되어 있습니다. 하지만 정말 그럴까요?

시험이라는 형식은 항상 한계를 가지고 있습니다. 그것은 어떤 면에서건 실전과는 다르기 때문이죠. 그렇다면 토익시험의 한계는 무엇일까요? 어떤 파트이건 간에 읽기 능력이 선행되어야 한다는 것입니다. 마치 우리가 수학문제나 사회 문제를 풀 때도 국어실력이 선행되어야 하는 것과 비슷하죠.

머리말

예를 들어 LC 문제인 파트 3과 4를 생각해보죠. 얼핏 듣기시험은 것 같지만 사실은 읽기 능력에 절반 이상 의존하고 있습니다. 듣기 문제가 방송되기 전에 빠른 속도로 문제를 먼저 읽어내야만 고득점이 가능하기 때문이죠. RC 문제인 파트 5, 6, 7은 말할 것도 없습니다. 결국, 파트 1, 2를 제외한 상대적으로 중요한 파트는 모두 읽기능력에 의해 좌우되는 셈입니다.

이 책은 파트 7에 등장하는 지문 형식으로만 쓰여 있습니다. 그러나 이 책이 전달하려는 내용은 파트 7에 한정되지 않습니다. 단어 때문에 읽기가 막혔을 때 어떻게 대처할 것인가가 바로 이 책이 전달하려는 내용이니까요.

그렇다면 토익시험이 가장 원하는 능력은 무엇일까요?

그것은 바로 '**단어를 몰라도 읽어내는 습관**'이 아닐까요?

Unit 001-004
Preview

Unit1-a

We must interrupt your service.
우리는 당신의 서비스를 중단해야만 합니다.

지불금을 받지 않는 한
Unless we receive a payment

we must interrupt your service.

Unless we receive a payment

9월 11일까지 55달러의
of $55 by September11,

we must interrupt your service.

Unit1-b

We will discontinue your service.
우리는 당신의 서비스를 중단할 겁니다.

만약 우리가 지불금을 받지 못하면
If we don't receive payment

we will discontinue your service.

If we don't receive payment

중단 후 10일 이내에
within 10 days after interruption,

we will discontinue your service.

8

Unit1-c

Please call us.
저희에게 전화 주세요.

질문이 있으면
If you have any questions

please call us.

If you have any questions

당신의 청구서 혹은 이 공지에 관한
concerning your bill or this notice,

please call us.

Unit2-a

Use the gate.
출입구를 사용하세요.

Use the gate

빌딩의 다른 방향에 있는
on the other side of the building.

빌딩에 들어올 때
When you enter the building,

use the gate on the other side of the building.

Unit 001-004
Preview

Unit2-b

All staff has permission.
전 직원은 권한을 가지고 있습니다.

All staff has permission

주차장 C를 사용하는
to use the parking lot C.

All staff has permission to use the parking lot C

수리가 진행되는 동안
while the renovation is being carried out.

Unit3-a

We are glad to announce.
알려드려서 기쁩니다.

We are glad to announce

운동 수업이 있으리라는 것을
that there will be exercise classes.

We are glad to announce that there will be exercise classes

직원들을 위한
for all employees.

We are glad to announce that there will be exercise classes for all employees

3월 1일에 시작하는
beginning the first of March.

Unit3-b

All should refer.
모두는 참고해야 합니다.

All

이 프로그램에 참가하기를 희망하는
those wishing to take part in this program

should refer.

All those wishing to take part in this program should refer

자세한 일정을
to the detailed schedule.

All those wishing to take part in this program should refer to the detailed schedule

게시판에 있는
on the bulletin board.

Unit 001–004
Preview

Unit3-c

All participants should fill out a health form and must have a health exam.

모든 참가자들은 건강 양식을 작성해야 하고 건강 검진을 받아야 합니다.

All participants should fill out a health form and must have a health exam

써니 힐 센터에서
in Sunny Hill Center.

All participants should fill out a health form

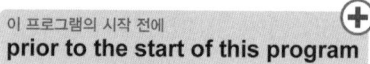
이 프로그램의 시작 전에
prior to the start of this program

and must have a health exam in Sunny Hill Center.

Unit4-a

Our company will now provide a shuttle service.

우리 회사에서는 이제 셔틀 버스 서비스를 제공할 것입니다.

Our company will now provide a shuttle service

시카고와 미시건 지점 사무실 사이에
between the Chicago and the Michigan branch office.

계속되는 직원들의 요청에 호응하여
In response to repeated requests from our employees,

our company will now provide a shuttle service between the Chicago and the Michigan branch office.

Unit 001-004
Preview

Unit4-b All information will be posted.
모든 정보는 게시될 것입니다.

All information will be posted

회사 웹사이트에
on the company website.

All information will be posted on the company website

5월 20일에
on May 20.

All information

서비스에 관한
regarding the service

will be posted on the company website on May 20.

All information regarding the service

노선과 요금을 포함하여
including routes and fares

will be posted on the company website on May 20.

Unit4-c

Employees are also encouraged.
직원들은 또한 장려됩니다.

Employees are also encouraged

카풀을 하기를
to carpool.

Employees are also encouraged to carpool

셔틀 서비스가 시작 하기까지
until the shuttle begins.

Unit 01

The due date on your bill has passed and we haven't received your payment. Unless we receive a payment of $55 by September 11, we must interrupt your service. If interrupted, you will be charged $20 for reconnection. Service will be restored within 24 hours. We will also

request an additional deposit. If we don't receive pay-
요구　　　　추가 보증금

ment within 10 days after interruption, we will discon-
　　　　중단 후 10일 이내에　　　　　　중단 할 것이다

tinue your service. If you decide to resume service later,
　　　　　　　　　　결정하다　재계할

a reinstallation charge of $40 will apply. If you have any
　　재설치 비용　　　　　적용할 것이다

questions concerning your bill or this notice, please call
　　　　~에 관한

us.

Unit 01

The due date on your bill has passed and we haven't received your payment. Unless we receive a payment of $55 by September 11, we must interrupt your service. If interrupted, you will be charged $20 for reconnection. Service will be restored within 24 hours. We will also request an additional deposit. If we don't receive payment within 10 days after interruption, we will discontinue your service. If you decide to resume service later, a reinstallation charge of $40 will apply. If you have any questions concerning your bill or this notice, please call us.

Unit 02

To: All staff
From: Maintenance department
Date: July 17

Please note that we have decided to renovate the first-floor lobby. This will take place on Friday, July 22 from 6 a.m. until 6 p.m. Employees won't be able to use the

main entrance while the construction crew is working.
정문 　　　　　　　　　　공사 인부들이 일하는 동안
When you enter the building, use the gate on the other
　　　　　　　　　　　　　　　　　　　다른 방향
side of the building. All staff has permission to use the
　　　　　　　　　　　전직원
parking lot C while the renovation is being carried out.
주차장　　　　　　　　수리가 진행되는 동안
Thank you for your cooperation. We apologize for this
　　　　　　　　협력　　　　　　　　사과하다
inconvenience.
불편

Unit 02

To: All staff

From: Maintenance department

Date: July 17

Please note that we have decided to renovate the first-floor lobby. This will take place on Friday, July 22 from 6 a.m. until 6 p.m. Employees won't be able to use the main entrance while the construction crew is working. When you enter the building, use the gate on the other side of the building. All staff has permission to use the parking lot C while the renovation is being carried out. Thank you for your cooperation. We apologize for this inconvenience.

Unit 03

From: Alex Shapiro
　　　　(이름)

To: All employees
　　모든 직원들

Re: Exercise classes
　　운동 강좌

We are glad to announce that there will be exercise classes for all employees beginning the first of March. The classes will take place in the company gym, which is located next to the cafeteria, from 7a.m. to 8a.m. daily. All employees are eligible to take classes free of charge. All those wishing to take part in this program should refer to the detailed schedule on the bulletin board. All are advised to register for the classes in advance. Optional exercise mats will be available for purchase in the employee cafeteria. All participants should fill out a health form prior to the start of this program and must have a health exam in Sunny Hill Center.

Unit 03

From: Alex Shapiro

To: All employees

Re: Exercise classes

We are glad to announce that there will be exercise classes for all employees beginning the first of March. The classes will take place in the company gym, which is located next to the cafeteria, from 7a.m. to 8a.m. daily. All employees are eligible to take classes free of charge.

All those wishing to take part in this program should refer to the detailed schedule on the bulletin board. All are advised to register for the classes in advance.

Optional exercise mats will be available for purchase in the employee cafeteria. All participants should fill out a health form prior to the start of this program and must have a health exam in Sunny Hill Center.

Unit 04

In response to repeated requests from our employees,
호응하여   계속되는 요청에   직원들

our company will now provide a shuttle service between
바로 제공할 것이다

the Chicago and the Michigan branch office. The current
(도시명)   (도시명)   지점 사무실

shuttle service from local train and bus stations will be
지역 기차와 버스역의

unaffected by this change.
영향을 받지 않을 것이다   변화

The new shuttle service will commence operation June
시작될 것이다   운행을   6월1일에

1st and fees will be charged. All information regarding the service including routes and fares will be posted on the company website on May 20. Please check it for future reference. To use the shuttle service, you must make a reservation two days in advance. Employees are also encouraged to carpool until the shuttle begins.

Unit 04

In response to repeated requests from our employees, our company will now provide a shuttle service between the Chicago and the Michigan branch office. The current shuttle service from local train and bus stations will be unaffected by this change.

The new shuttle service will commence operation June

1st and fees will be charged. All information regarding the service including routes and fares will be posted on the company website on May 20. Please check it for future reference. To use the shuttle service, you must make a reservation two days in advance. Employees are also encouraged to carpool until the shuttle begins.

Unit 005-008
Preview

Unit5-a

New Orleans public officials cordially invite all citizens.

뉴 올리언즈 공무원들은 진심으로 모든 시민들을 초대합니다.

New Orleans public officials cordially invite all citizens

참석하도록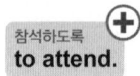
to attend.

New Orleans public officials cordially invite all citizens to attend

이번 달 회의에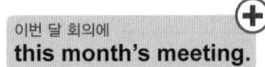
this month's meeting.

New Orleans public officials cordially invite all citizens to attend this month's meeting,

시민회관에서 이뤄지는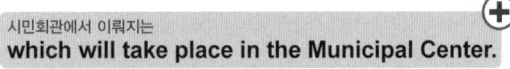
which will take place in the Municipal Center.

Unit5-b

We request.
저희는 요청합니다.

We request

> 가족들이 스스로 제한하는 것을
> **that families limit themselves.**

We request that families limit themselves

> 한 가구당 한 명으로
> **to one head per household.**

> 제한된 좌석 때문에
> **due to limited seating,**

we request that families limit themselves to one head per household.

> 비록 모든 분들이 이 회의에 참석하는 것을 환영하기는 하지만,
> **Although anyone is welcome to attend this meeting,**

due to limited seating, we request that families limit themselves to one head per household.

Unit 005-008
Preview

Unit5-c

Of particular importance is
특히 중요한 것은 ~라는 점입니다.

Of particular importance is

날씨 문제를 어떻게 대처할 것인가
how to deal with weather problems.

Of particular importance is how to deal with weather problems

허리케인과 같은
like hurricanes.

Of particular importance is how to deal with weather problems like hurricanes,

도시가 비용을 더 지불해야 하는
which require the city to spend more.

Of particular importance is how to deal with weather problems like hurricanes, which require the city to spend more.

도로 정비에
on road maintenance.

Unit5-d

City officials would like to survey citizens.

시 공무원들은 시민들에게 설문 조사 하기를 원합니다.

City officials would like to survey citizens

가장 필수적인 사안들에 동의하기 전에
before agreeing on the most essential.

많은 건설 프로젝트들이 있습니다만
There are many construction projects, but

city officials would like to survey citizens before agreeing on the most essential.

There are many construction projects

다가오는 년도에 계획된
planned for the upcoming year,

but city officials would like to survey citizens before agreeing on the most essential.

Unit 005-008
Preview

Unit6-a

The nation's top home appliance distributor is currently seeking a qualified candidate.

국내 최고의 가전 업계 배급업자는 현재 자격 있는 지원자를 찾고 있습니다.

The nation's top home appliance distributor

파라곤 주식회사는
, Paragon Inc.,

is currently seeking a qualified candidate.

The nation's top home appliance distributor, Paragon Inc., is currently seeking a qualified candidate

제품 개발자로써 일할
to work as a product developer.

The nation's top home appliance distributor, Paragon Inc., is currently seeking a qualified candidate to work as a product developer

미네아폴리스 사무실에서
in its Minneapolis office.

Unit6-b

Candidates must possess a strong background and have some experience.

지원자들은 탄탄한 배경지식을 소유해야 하고 경험이 있어야 합니다.

Candidates must possess a strong background and have some experience

제품에 관하여 일한
working with products.

Candidates must possess a strong background and have some experience working with products

소매를 의도하는
intended for retail sale.

Unit 005–008
Preview

Candidates must possess a strong background

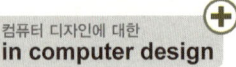
컴퓨터 디자인에 대한
in computer design

and have some experience working with products intended for retail sale.

Unit7-a

We feel fortunate.
저희는 행운을 느낍니다.

We feel fortunate

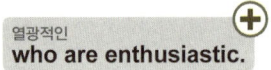
아주 멋진 직원들과 함께 한다는
to have such a wonderful group of employees.

We feel fortunate to have such a wonderful group of employees

열광적인
who are enthusiastic.

We feel fortunate to have such a wonderful group of employees who are enthusiastic

회사 행사에 참석하는 것에 대해
about attending company functions.

Unit7-b

Sign-up sheets will be posted.
신청서는 놓여질 것입니다.

Sign-up sheets will be posted

직원 휴게실에
in the employee break room.

Sign-up sheets will be posted in the employee break room

지금부터 모레까지
from now until the day after tomorrow.

Unit 005-008
Preview

Unit8-a

I have been talking to the members, and we think.

저는 멤버들과 얘기해왔으며, 우리는 생각합니다.

I have been talking to the members, and we think

농구를 하는 것은 A일 뿐 아니라 B라고
that playing basketball would not only A but B.

I have been talking to the members, and we think that playing basketball

회사 야유회에서의
at the company picnic

would not only A but B.

I have been talking to the members, and we think that playing basketball at the company picnic would

재미 있을 뿐 아니라 다른 직원들도 장려하게 될 것입니다
not only be fun but may encourage additional employees.

I have been talking to the members, and we think that playing basketball at the company picnic would not only be fun

가족들에게
for families

but may encourage additional employees.

I have been talking to the members, and we think that playing basketball at the company picnic would not only be fun for families but may encourage additional employees

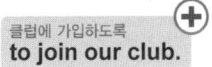
클럽에 가입하도록
to join our club.

Unit 05

New Orleans public officials cordially invite all citizens to attend this month's meeting, which will take place in the Municipal Center. Although anyone is welcome to attend this meeting, due to limited seating, we request that families limit themselves to one head per household.

Last month, the meeting discussed important issues such as the public library renovation, the annual art festival. This month, however, we would like to focus on short term issues, like disaster relief services and emergency funds. Of particular importance is how to deal with weather problems like hurricanes, which require the city to spend more on road maintenance. There are many construction projects planned for the upcoming year, but city officials would like to survey citizens before agreeing on the most essential.

Unit 05

New Orleans public officials cordially invite all citizens to attend this month's meeting, which will take place in the Municipal Center. Although anyone is welcome to attend this meeting, due to limited seating, we request that families limit themselves to one head per household.

Last month, the meeting discussed important issues such as the public library renovation, the annual art festival. This month, however, we would like to focus on short term issues, like disaster relief services and emergency funds. Of particular importance is how to deal with weather problems like hurricanes, which require the city to spend more on road maintenance. There are many construction projects planned for the upcoming year, but city officials would like to survey citizens before agreeing on the most essential.

Unit 06

The nation's top home appliance distributor, Paragon Inc., is currently seeking a qualified candidate to work as a product developer in its Minneapolis office. The position will require extensive travel to Paragon's main office in Los Angeles to affiliate offices in Frankfurt and Sao Paolo. The product developer will be responsible for coming up with new products and finding ways to enhance existing products. Candidates must possess a strong background in computer design and have some experience working with products intended for retail sale. Only university graduates will be considered and familiarity with the home appliance industry will be highly regarded. Applicants with at least two years of design experience are preferred. Excellent pay and fringe benefits will be offered.

Please mail a copy of your resume and cover letter, along with a letter of reference no later than March 24. Applications by e-mail will not be accepted

Unit 06

The nation's top home appliance distributor, Paragon Inc., is currently seeking a qualified candidate to work as a product developer in its Minneapolis office. The position will require extensive travel to Paragon's main office in Los Angeles to affiliate offices in Frankfurt and Sao Paolo. The product developer will be responsible for coming up with new products and finding ways to enhance existing products. Candidates must possess a strong background in computer design and have some experience working with products intended for retail sale. Only university graduates will be considered and familiarity with the home appliance industry will be highly regarded. Applicants with at least two years of design experience are preferred. Excellent pay and fringe benefits will be offered.

Please mail a copy of your resume and cover letter, along with a letter of reference no later than March 24. Applications by e-mail will not be accepted

Unit 07

To: All employees
From: Andrew Scholes
Date: November 25

Subject: Annual picnic

It's time again for our annual picnic. We feel fortunate to have such a wonderful group of employees who are enthusiastic about attending company functions. This year's picnic will be held on Saturday, November 30, from 11 a.m. to 4 p.m. at Hancock Park, the same place it was held last year.

The company will be providing food, beverages, musical entertainment, and a variety of children's games. Sign-up sheets will be posted in the employee break room from now until the day after tomorrow. If you plan to attend the picnic, you must sign up in order to be issued a ticket.

Our management team welcomes this opportunity for all of us to gather as a group. We look forward to seeing you at Hancock Park.

Best regards,

Andrew Scholes

Unit 07

To: All employees

From: Andrew Scholes

Date: November 25

Subject: Annual picnic

It's time again for our annual picnic. We feel fortunate to have such a wonderful group of employees who are enthusiastic about attending company functions. This year's picnic will be held on Saturday, November 30, from 11 a.m. to 4 p.m. at Hancock Park, the same place it was held last year.

The company will be providing food, beverages, musical entertainment, and a variety of children's games. Sign-up sheets will be posted in the employee break room from now until the day after tomorrow. If you plan to attend the picnic, you must sign up in order to be issued a ticket.

Our management team welcomes this opportunity for all of us to gather as a group. We look forward to seeing you at Hancock Park.

Best regards,

Andrew Scholes

Unit 08

Dear Mr. Scholes,
　　　(이름)

Thanks to your suggestion, we have recently formed
　　　　　　　제안　　　　　　　최근에 구성 되어졌다

a company basketball club. About fifteen people have
　　사내 농구 클럽

joined so far, and we have been playing basketball at
지금까지 합류했다　　　　　　　농구를 해오고 있다

Grace Park every Sunday for the last few months. I have
(공원명)　　　　　　　　지난 몇 달 동안

been talking to the members, and we think that playing
회원들에게 말해왔다

basketball at the company picnic would not only be fun
회사 야유회에서의 농구 하기는   재미 있을 뿐 아니라
for families but may encourage additional employees to
장려도 하게 될 것이다   추가 직원들이
join our club. However, if I remember correctly from last
우리 클럽에 합류하도록   만약 내가 정확하게 기억한다면
year, there were no basketball courts at the park. Would
농구장이 없었다
you consider holding the picnic at Grace Park this year?
고려하다   야유회를 개최하다
If you are willing to consider this, I would be happy to
고려할 것이다   기꺼이 확인하겠다
check the availability of Grace Park.
가능성

Unit 08

Dear Mr. Scholes,

Thanks to your suggestion, we have recently formed a company basketball club. About fifteen people have joined so far, and we have been playing basketball at Grace Park every Sunday for the last few months. I have been talking to the members, and we think that playing basketball at the company picnic would not only be fun for families but may encourage additional employees to join our club. However, if I remember correctly from last year, there were no basketball courts at the park. Would you consider holding the picnic at Grace Park this year? If you are willing to consider this, I would be happy to check the availability of Grace Park.

Unit 009-012
Preview

Unit9-a

Rene's leadership has helped.
Rene의 리더십은 도움이 되었습니다.

Rene's leadership has helped

다른 여러 종류의 상들과 퓰리처 상을 우리가 받을 수 있도록
bring us a Pulitzer Prize and a long list of other honors.

Rene's leadership

뉴욕 포스트 팀의
of the New York Post team

has helped bring us a Pulitzer Prize and a long list of other honors.

Rene's leadership of the New York Post team,

신문 부서들 중 가장 크고 강력한 조사 활동을 하는
the largest and most powerful investigative operation of any newspaper bureau

has helped bring us a Pulitzer Prize and a long list of other honors.

Unit9-b

We will organize several opportunities.

우리는 몇몇의 기회를 준비할 것입니다.

We will organize several opportunities

Rene의 안녕을 고하기 위해
to bid Rene's farewell.

We will organize several opportunities to bid Rene's farewell

그녀가 떠나는 날이 다가옴에 따라
as her departure approaches.

Unit 009-012
Preview

Unit10-a

It is detrimental to the company.
회사에 대한 손해입니다.

It is detrimental to the company

A가 B를 하는 것은
for A to B.

It is detrimental to the company

많은 직원이 B하는 것은
for so many employees to B.

It is detrimental to the company for so many employees

동시에 휴가를 사용하는 것은
to take days off at the same time.

그것들은 개인적인 월차 휴가이고 우리는 한계를 설정하고 싶지 않긴 하지만,

While they are your personal days and we would like to set no boundaries,

it is detrimental to the company for so many employees to take days off at the same time.

While they are your personal days and we would like to set no boundaries

월차를 사용하도록 허가 되는 때에
on when you are allowed to take them,

it is detrimental to the company for so many employees to take days off at the same time.

Unit 009-012
Preview

Unit10-b

It is almost impossible to perform.
행하는 것은 거의 불가능합니다.

It is almost impossible to perform

몇몇 일들을
some of the tasks.

It is almost impossible to perform some of the tasks

해야 할 필요가 있는
that need to be done.

이렇게 적은 숫자의 직원들로는
With such low numbers of employees

it is almost impossible to perform some of the tasks that need to be done.

With such low numbers of employees

출근하는
reporting to work

it is almost impossible to perform some of the tasks that need to be done.

Unit10-c

We will have no alternative but to institute.

우리는 대안이 없어서 도입할 것이다.

We will have no alternative but to institute

월차의 정해진 순번을
a scheduled rotation of personal days.

만약 이 추세가 혹시라도 계속된다면,
If this trend persists by any chance,

we will have no alternative but to institute a scheduled rotation of personal days.

우리는 어떤 규정을 부과하는 것을 꺼리지만,
We are reluctant to impose any rules, however,

if this trend persists by any chance, we will have no alternative but to institute a scheduled rotation of personal days.

Unit 009-012
Preview

We are reluctant to impose any rules

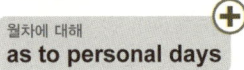
월차에 대해
as to personal days

however, if this trend persists by any chance, we will have no alternative but to institute a scheduled rotation of personal days.

We are reluctant to impose any rules as to personal days

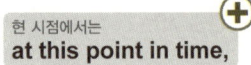
현 시점에서는
at this point in time,

however, if this trend persists by any chance, we will have no alternative but to institute a scheduled rotation of personal days.

Unit11-a

We will assume responsibility.
우리는 책임질 것입니다.

만약 제품이 오작동하면
Should the product malfunction,

we will assume responsibility.

Should the product malfunction, we will assume responsibility

수리에 대한 비용을
for the cost of the repairs.

Should the product malfunction

기계적인 결함 때문에
due to a mechanical defect

we will assume responsibility for the cost of the repairs.

Should the product malfunction

구매한 날부터 5년 이내에
within 5 years of the date of purchase

due to a mechanical defect, we will assume responsibility for the cost of the repairs.

Unit 009-012
Preview

Unit11-b

The centers are equipped.
서비스 센터들은 (장비가) 준비되어 있습니다.

The centers are equipped

최신식의 장비들로
with state-of-the-art equipment.

The centers are equipped with state-of-the-art equipment

고객들에게 제공하기 위한
to provide our customers.

The centers are equipped with state-of-the-art equipment to provide our customers

다양한 수리와 서비스들을
with a wide variety of repairs and services.

The centers are equipped with state-of-the-art equipment to provide our customers with a wide variety of repairs and services

Superior의 전문가적 기준에 따라서 행해지는
that are performed according to Superior's professional standards.

Unit12-a

Detailed information is described.
상세한 정보는 설명되어 있습니다.

Detailed information

복지에 관한
on benefits

is described.

Unit 009-012
Preview

Detailed information on benefits is described

동봉된 개요에
in the enclosed summary.

Detailed information on benefits is described in the enclosed summary

정직원 체계 안내서의
of full-time employee programs brochure.

Unit12-b Please contact the Human Resources Department and schedule your employment and benefits processing.

인사과에 전화해 주시고 고용과 복지 절차의 일정을 잡으세요.

Please contact the Human Resources Department

이 지위를 받아들이기 위해
to accept this position

and schedule your employment and benefits processing.

Please contact the Human Resources Department to accept this position and schedule your employment and benefits processing

일반적인 오리엔테이션 절차 이외에도
in addition to your general orientation.

Please contact the Human Resources Department to accept this position and schedule your employment and benefits processing in addition to your general orientation

626-441-3234, 내선번호 555로
at 626-441-3234, ext. 555.

Unit 09

To: Team Members
From: Shane Barkley, editor-in-chief
Re: René Stein

Dear Colleagues:

I am very sorry to report that René Stein, who has brilliantly led our investigative team for 23 years, will be leaving us in September for a teaching job at the University of North Carolina.

René's leadership of the New York Post team, the largest and most powerful investigative operation of any newspaper bureau, has helped bring us a Pulitzer Prize

and a long list of other honors.
North Carolina has wooed her away with a job that René says is exactly what she has always wanted to do: She will be teaching investigative reporting at one of the country's best journalism schools and launching a new program under the Armstrong Journalism Program, the Armstrong Corporation's ambitious effort to improve journalism education nationwide.
Her departure will be a huge loss for us, but we know it is good for her. We will organize several opportunities to bid René's farewell as her departure approaches.

Unit 09

To: Team Members

From: Shane Barkley, editor-in-chief

Re: René Stein

Dear Colleagues:

I am very sorry to report that René Stein, who has brilliantly led our investigative team for 23 years, will be leaving us in September for a teaching job at the University of North Carolina.

René's leadership of the New York Post team, the largest and most powerful investigative operation of any newspaper bureau, has helped bring us a Pulitzer Prize and a long list of other honors.

North Carolina has wooed her away with a job that René says is exactly what she has always wanted to do: She will be teaching investigative reporting at one of the country's best journalism schools and launching a new program under the Armstrong Journalism Program, the Armstrong Corporation's ambitious effort to improve journalism education nationwide.

Her departure will be a huge loss for us, but we know it is good for her. We will organize several opportunities to bid René's farewell as her departure approaches.

Unit 10

To: All employees

From: General Management

It has come to our attention that there has been a significant rise in the number of personal days employees have been taking over the past six months. While they are your personal days and we would like to set no boundaries on when you are allowed to take them, it is detrimental to the company for so many employees to take days off at the same time. Last month alone, the Accounting Department reported that between 30%

and 40% of their staff took personal days on Fridays. With such low numbers of employees reporting to work it is almost impossible to perform some of the tasks that need to be done. We are reluctant to impose any rules as to personal days at this point in time, however, if this trend persists by any chance, we will have no alternative but to institute a scheduled rotation of personal days. Your cooperation on this matter would be highly appreciated.

Sincerely,

Jimmy Rollins

Unit 10

To: All employees

From: General Management

It has come to our attention that there has been a significant rise in the number of personal days employees have been taking over the past six months. While they are your personal days and we would like to set no boundaries on when you are allowed to take them, it is detrimental to the company for so many employees to take days off at the same time. Last month alone, the Accounting Department reported that between 30%

and 40% of their staff took personal days on Fridays. With such low numbers of employees reporting to work it is almost impossible to perform some of the tasks that need to be done.

We are reluctant to impose any rules as to personal days at this point in time, however, if this trend persists by any chance, we will have no alternative but to institute a scheduled rotation of personal days. Your cooperation on this matter would be highly appreciated.

Sincerely,

Jimmy Rollins

Unit 11

Thank you for purchasing the superior camera. Our long-established reputation for quality and customer service and our long history of providing fine electronics to avid users around the world is a great source of pride. Superior cameras are made with the highest-quality materials available to maximize the performance of our products. However, should the product malfunction within 5 years of the date of purchase due to a mechanical defect, we will assume responsibility for the cost of the repairs. Please note, however, that this warranty covers the cost of parts and labor only. Shipping, insurance and batteries may not be claimed under this warranty. In the event that the product requires repair or some other service, please take or ship it to one of the Superior's authorized service centers. The centers are equipped with state-of-the-art equipment to provide our customers with a wide variety of repairs and services that are performed according to Superior's professional standards. Please see the enclosed list of authorized Superior distributors and service centers in your country.

Unit 11

Thank you for purchasing the superior camera. Our long-established reputation for quality and customer service and our long history of providing fine electronics to avid users around the world is a great source of pride. Superior cameras are made with the highest-quality materials available to maximize the performance of our products. However, should the product malfunction within 5 years of the date of purchase due to a mechanical defect, we will assume responsibility for the cost of the repairs. Please note, however, that this warranty covers the cost of parts and labor only. Shipping, insurance and batteries may not be claimed under this warranty.

In the event that the product requires repair or some other service, please take or ship it to one of the Superior's authorized service centers. The centers are equipped with state-of-the-art equipment to provide our customers with a wide variety of repairs and services that are performed according to Superior's professional standards. Please see the enclosed list of authorized Superior distributors and service centers in your country.

Unit 12

Dear Irene Boyle,
　　　(이름)

Congratulations! This letter is to inform you that you have been accepted into the Overseas Sales department manager position at Thomson Corporation. Your annual starting salary will be $80,000. Detailed information on benefits is described in the enclosed summary of full-time employee programs brochure. The particulars of these programs will be discussed during your employment orientation.

We have scheduled your first day for March 2. Please

contact the Human Resources Department to accept this position and schedule your employment and benefits processing in addition to your general orientation at 626-441-3234, ext 555.

Don't hesitate to call me with any questions you may have / regarding your employment here. In the meantime, we look forward to you joining the staff and the positive contributions we believe you will make at Thomson Corporation.

Sincerely,

Vitally Henry

Unit 12

Dear Irene Boyle,

Congratulations! This letter is to inform you that you have been accepted into the Overseas Sales department manager position at Thomson Corporation.

Your annual starting salary will be $80,000. Detailed information on benefits is described in the enclosed summary of full-time employee programs brochure. The particulars of these programs will be discussed during your employment orientation.

We have scheduled your first day for March 2. Please

contact the Human Resources Department to accept this position and schedule your employment and benefits processing in addition to your general orientation at 626-441-3234, ext 555.

Don't hesitate to call me with any questions you may have / regarding your employment here. In the meantime, we look forward to you joining the staff and the positive contributions we believe you will make at Thomson Corporation.

Sincerely,

Vitally Henry

Unit 013-016
Preview

Unit13-a

You can A, B, and C.
당신은 A, B, 그리고 C를 할 수 있습니다.

You can

당신은 티켓을 구매 혹은 예약할 수 있고, 정보를 찾을 수 있으며, 그리고 지역의 철도노선을 얻을 수 있습니다.
purchase or reserve tickets, find information, and get regional rail maps.

You can purchase or reserve tickets

사전에 웹사이트를 통해
in advance through the website,

find information, and get regional rail maps.

You can purchase or reserve tickets in advance through the website, find information

지방 도로에 교통정체에 관한
about traffic delays on local roads

and get regional rail maps.

You can purchase or reserve tickets in advance through the website, find information about traffic delays on local roads, and get regional rail maps

더 편리하게 만들기 위해
to make it more convenient.

You can purchase or reserve tickets in advance through the website, find information about traffic delays on local roads, and get regional rail maps to make it more convenient

당신이 여행을 계획하는데 있어
for you to plan your travel.

Unit13-b

Our website will display time estimates.

저희 웹사이트는 추정 시간을 표시할 것입니다.

Our website will display time estimates

서비스에 대한
for service.

Unit 013-016
Preview

Our website will display time estimates for service

복구 될
to be restored.

드물지만 일이 일어나는 경우
In the rare event,

our website will display time estimates for service to be restored.

In the rare event

주요 서비스가 중단 되는
of a major service interruption,

our website will display time estimates for service to be restored.

In the rare event of a major service interruption

하나 또는 이상의 차선에서
on one or more train lines,

our website will display time estimates for service to be restored.

Unit13-c

Please feel free to e-mail.
언제든지 이메일 하세요.

Please feel free to e-mail

어떤 질문이나 제안이든
any questions or suggestions.

Please feel free to e-mail any questions or suggestions

당신이 가질지 모르는
you might have.

Please feel free to e-mail any questions or suggestions you might have

이 메일 주소로
to info@mtrail.com.

Unit 013-016
Preview

Unit14-a

The accommodation options shall match.
숙소의 옵션들은 부합할 것입니다.

The accommodation options shall match

당신의 원하는 선택에 ➕
with your preferred choice.

The accommodation options shall match with your preferred choice

당신이 이메일에 언급했던 ➕
that you had mentioned in your email.

The accommodation options

아래에 작성된 ➕
listed below

shall match with your preferred choice that you had mentioned in your email.

Unit14-b

2-year lease, renewable, lovely 4-bedroom house.

2년 임대차 계약, 연장 가능한 사랑스러운 4개의 방이 있는 집.

2-year lease, renewable, lovely 4-bedroom house

근처에 위치한
located in the vicinity.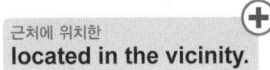

2-year lease, renewable, lovely 4-bedroom house located in the vicinity

학교와 공원, 쇼핑센터의
of the shopping center, park and school.

Unit15-a

The first of four training sessions began.

네 가지 교육 과정 중 첫 번째가 시작됐습니다.

수요일에
On Wednesday,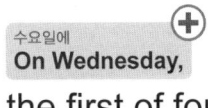

the first of four training sessions began.

Unit 013-016
Preview

On Wednesday, the first of four training sessions began

록펠러 컨벤션 센터에서
at Rockefeller Convention Center.

On Wednesday, the first of four training sessions began at Rockefeller Convention Center

컨벤션 센터 직원들에게 가르치기 위해
to teach convention center workers.

On Wednesday, the first of four training sessions began at Rockefeller Convention Center to teach convention center workers

어떻게 최고의 서비스를 제공할 수 있는지
how to deliver first-class service.

On Wednesday, the first of four training sessions began at Rockefeller Convention Center to teach convention center workers how to deliver first-class service

미팅 기획자들과 전시자들에게
to meeting planners and exhibitors.

Unit15-b

Participants will be eligible for gift certificates.

참가자들은 상품권을 가질 수 있을 것입니다.

Participants will be eligible for gift certificates

지역 상점이나 식당의
to local stores and restaurants.

직원들에게 권장하기 위해
To encourage employees,

participants will be eligible for gift certificates to local stores and restaurants.

Unit 013-016
Preview

To encourage employees

교육 과정에 등록하도록 ⊕
to sign up for the training sessions

participants will be eligible for gift certificates to local stores and restaurants.

Unit15-c

I also wanted to say.
저는 또한 말하고 싶습니다.

I also wanted to say

상품권에 감사하다고 ⊕
that I appreciate the gift voucher.

I also wanted to say that I appreciate the gift voucher

Gecko's Garden 의 ⊕
to the Gecko's Garden.

Unit16-a

The person will work directly.
그 사람은 바로 일할 것입니다.

The person

hired (고용된)

will work directly.

The person hired will work directly
under the supervision. (감독 하에)

The person hired will work directly under the supervision
of the senior programmer. (선임 프로그래머의)

Unit 013-016
Preview

Unit16-b

The person must A, B, and must be willing to work.
그 사람은 반드시 A,B 여야 하고 기꺼이 근무해야 합니다.

The person must

팀으로 일을 잘 하고, 문제 해결을 잘 해야 하고 ⊕
**work well in a team,
be a good problem solver,**

and must be willing to work.

The person must work well in a team, be a good problem solver, and must be willing to work

야근과 주말근무를 ⊕
some evenings and weekends.

The person must work well in a team, be a good problem solver, and must be willing to work some evenings and weekends

필요하면 프로젝트가 빨리 완성될 수 있도록 ⊕
if necessary to push a project to completion.

Unit16-c

Please e-mail your resume.

당신의 이력서를 이메일로 보내주세요.

Please e-mail your resume,

일한 이력과 당신이 알고 있는 컴퓨터 언어를 포함하는
including previous work history and programming languages you know.

Please e-mail your resume, including previous work history and programming languages you know

인사부장 Brad Franklin에게
to the hiring manager, Brad Franklin.

Please e-mail your resume, including previous work history and programming languages you know to the hiring manager, Brad Franklin,

이 메일 주소로
at brad@centech.com.

Unit 13

Attention Train Passengers:

The Metro Transit Rail Service's recently redesigned website now offers a wider array of useful information. The site (www.mtrail.com) now lists all fares and train schedules, including those for weekends and holidays. You can purchase or reserve tickets in advance through the website, find information about traffic delays on local roads, and get regional rail maps to make it more convenient for you to plan your travel.

Any delays or service interruptions will be posted on the site, which will be continually updated. In the rare event of a major service interruption on one or more train lines, our website will display time estimates for service to be restored. We hope the enhanced website will make rail travel even more pleasant for you. We are always looking for ways to better serve our valued passengers. Please feel free to e-mail any questions or suggestions you might have to info@mtrail.com.

Unit 13

Attention Train Passengers:

The Metro Transit Rail Service's recently redesigned website now offers a wider array of useful information. The site (www.mtrail.com) now lists all fares and train schedules, including those for weekends and holidays. You can purchase or reserve tickets in advance through the website, find information about traffic delays on local roads, and get regional rail maps to make it more convenient for you to plan your travel.

Any delays or service interruptions will be posted on the site, which will be continually updated. In the rare event of a major service interruption on one or more train lines, our website will display time estimates for service to be restored.

We hope the enhanced website will make rail travel even more pleasant for you. We are always looking for ways to better serve our valued passengers. Please feel free to e-mail any questions or suggestions you might have to info@mtrail.com.

Unit 14

Top Real Estate

Re: Your inquiries

Dear Mrs. West,

Thank you for your inquiry. The accommodation options listed below shall match with your preferred choice that you had mentioned in your email. Please feel free to write to me for more information.

Location 1

Available from early January. 2-year lease, renewable, lovely 4-bedroom house located in the vicinity of the shopping center, park and school. New kitchen, spacious

patio and bathroom with Jacuzzi. Would be perfect for a
family of around 3 or more. No pets allowed.

Location 2
Beautiful 4-bedroom house **adjacent to the King College campus**. Perfect residential area. Beautifully furnished two-story house with spiral staircase. Available in February, big yard, pets allowed after pre-arrangement. Rent $2,000 per month

Location 3
Available now, 3-bedroom with a beautiful backyard in a calm suburban area. Spacious kitchen and living room. One-year contract, $1,700 per month including utilities.

Unit 14

Top Real Estate

Re: Your inquiries

Dear Mrs. West,

Thank you for your inquiry. The accommodation options listed below shall match with your preferred choice that you had mentioned in your email. Please feel free to write to me for more information.

Location 1

Available from early January. 2-year lease, renewable, lovely 4-bedroom house located in the vicinity of the shopping center, park and school. New kitchen, spacious patio and bathroom with Jacuzzi. Would be perfect for a family of around 3 or more. No pets allowed.

Location 2

Beautiful 4-bedroom house adjacent to the King College campus. Perfect residential area. Beautifully furnished two-story house with spiral staircase. Available in February, big yard, pets allowed after pre-arrangement. Rent $2,000 per month

Location 3

Available now, 3-bedroom with a beautiful backyard in a calm suburban area. Spacious kitchen and living room. One-year contract, $1,700 per month including utilities.

Unit 15

On Wednesday, the first of four training sessions began at Rockefeller Convention Center to teach convention center workers how to deliver first-class service to meeting planners and exhibitors. At the first two-hour session, consultant Brandon Donovan led sales managers and exhibition staff. On Thursday, food service workers participated in a similar training session with Brandon Donovan. The consultant will conduct the final two sessions next Monday and Tuesday.

In an interview, Brandon Donovan said, "For any business, it is important that its employees learn to treat customers with respect." To encourage employees to sign up for the training sessions, participants will be eligible for gift certificates to local stores and restaurants.

Re: Training sessions

Dear Mr. Donovan;

I just wanted to let you know that I enjoyed the training session last Thursday. I learned some useful ideas that will help me in my work. I also wanted to say that I appreciate the gift voucher to the Gecko's Garden.

Sincerely,

Steve Liu

Unit 15

On Wednesday, the first of four training sessions began at Rockefeller Convention Center to teach convention center workers how to deliver first-class service to meeting planners and exhibitors. At the first two-hour session, consultant Brandon Donovan led sales managers and exhibition staff. On Thursday, food service workers participated in a similar training session with Brandon Donovan. The consultant will conduct the final two sessions next Monday and Tuesday.

In an interview, Brandon Donovan said, "For any business, it is important that its employees learn to treat customers with respect." To encourage employees to sign up for the training sessions, participants will be eligible for gift certificates to local stores and restaurants.

Re: Training sessions

Dear Mr. Donovan;

I just wanted to let you know that I enjoyed the training session last Thursday. I learned some useful ideas that will help me in my work. I also wanted to say that I appreciate the gift voucher to the Gecko's Garden.

Sincerely,

Steve Liu

Unit 16

Century Tech, New York's leading technology firm, is currently hiring a full time programmer. The person hired will work directly under the supervision of the senior programmer. Initial duties will mainly include testing. As his and her experience develops, the person will be responsible for creating new programs and expanding existing programs. Century Tech offers a competitive salary and excellent opportunities for growth.

The applicant must hold a bachelor's degree in computer science and a related field and must be familiar with several programming languages. The person will work intensively with our preferred consulting firm, Ivy Grove Tech. The person must work well in a team, be a good problem solver, and must be willing to work some evenings and weekends if necessary to push a project to completion.

Please e-mail your resume, including previous work history and programming languages you know to the hiring manager, Brad Franklin, at brad@centech.com.

Unit 16

Century Tech, New York's leading technology firm, is currently hiring a full time programmer. The person hired will work directly under the supervision of the senior programmer. Initial duties will mainly include testing. As his and her experience develops, the person will be responsible for creating new programs and expanding existing programs. Century Tech offers a competitive salary and excellent opportunities for growth.

The applicant must hold a bachelor's degree in computer science and a related field and must be familiar with several programming languages. The person will work intensively with our preferred consulting firm, Ivy Grove Tech. The person must work well in a team, be a good problem solver, and must be willing to work some evenings and weekends if necessary to push a project to completion.

Please e-mail your resume, including previous work history and programming languages you know to the hiring manager, Brad Franklin, at brad@centech.com.

Unit 017-020
Preview

Unit17-a

We have a young programmer here.
여기 젊은 프로그래머가 있습니다.

We have a young programmer here

Britta Forsberg 라는 이름을 가진 ⊕
named Britta Forsberg.

We have a young programmer here named Britta Forsberg ⊕

우리와 함께하는 인턴십을 완료할
who will complete her internship with us.

We have a young programmer here named Britta Forsberg who will complete her internship with us

다음 달 말에 ⊕
at the end of next month.

Unit17-b

But Globemedia currently have no openings.

그러나 Globemedia는 현재 공석이 없습니다.

But Globemedia currently have no openings

예산 삭감과 채용 동결 때문에
due to budget cuts and a hiring freeze.

저는 그녀를 정규직으로 고용할 수 있길 원하지만
I would love to be able to hire her full time,

but Globemedia currently have no openings due to budget cuts and a hiring freeze.

Unit17-c

She has taken on increasing responsibilities, and she has become a person.

그녀는 증가하는 책임들을 떠맡았으며 그녀는 사람이 되었습니다.

Unit 017-020
Preview

She has taken on increasing responsibilities, and she has become a person

몇몇 상급 프로그래머들이 상담하는
some senior programmers consult.

She has taken on increasing responsibilities, and she has become a person some senior programmers consult

그들이 다른 의견을 원할 때
when they want a second opinion.

그녀가 있던 해에,
In the year she's been here,

she has taken on increasing responsibilities, and she has become a person some senior programmers consult when they want a second opinion.

Unit18-a

All of us wanted to let you know.
우리 모두 당신이 알게 되길 원했습니다.

All of us

여기 Andy 목재에 있는
here at Andy's lumber

wanted to let you know.

All of us here at Andy's lumber wanted to let you know

다가오는 이전과 확장에 관해서
about our upcoming relocation and expansion.

All of us here at Andy's lumber wanted to let you,

우리의 소중한 고객들 중의 한 명으로써
as one of our valued customers,

know about our upcoming relocation and expansion.

Unit 017-020
Preview

Unit18-b

We will soon be moving.
우리는 곧 이전할 것입니다.

We will soon be moving

더 큰 시설로
to a bigger facility.

We will soon be moving to a bigger facility

Tacoma에 있는
in Tacoma.

We will soon be moving to a bigger facility in Tacoma

우리의 공급업체에 가까워 지도록
so that we may be closer to our suppliers.

Unit18-c

The facility will also have a bigger parking lot.
점포는 또한 더 큰 주차장을 가지게 될 것입니다.

The facility will also have a bigger parking lot

간편한 적재를 위해서 ⊕
for convenient loading.

The facility will also have a bigger parking lot

영업장 바로 옆에 위치한 ⊕
located right next to the sales area

for convenient loading.

Unit19-a

The human resources department will be holding.

인사과는 개최할 것입니다.

The human resources department will be holding

이번 달에 다음의 설명회를 ⊕
the following information sessions this month.

Unit 017-020
Preview

The human resources department will be holding the following information sessions this month

다음과 같이
as follows:

성공적인 한 해의 시작을 용이하게 하기 위해
To facilitate a successful start to the year,

the human resources department will be holding the following information sessions this month as follows:

Unit20-a

The director recently sent you an e-mail.
부장님이 근래에 당신에게 이메일을 보냈습니다.

The director recently sent you an e-mail

다양한 설명회가 나열된
that lists the various information sessions.

The director recently sent you an e-mail that lists the various information sessions

이번 달에 제공되고 있는
being offered this month.

The director

인사과의
of the human resources department

recently sent you an e-mail that lists the various information sessions being offered this month.

Unit20-b

Please note that attendance is mandatory.

참석이 의무적이라는 것을 유의하세요.

Please note that attendance is mandatory

모두에게
for everyone.

Unit 017-020
Preview

Please note that attendance

3월 8일 설명회에서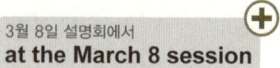
at the March 8 session

is mandatory for everyone.

Please note that attendance at the March 8 session is mandatory for everyone

단지 신입 사원뿐 아니라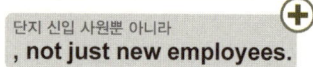
, not just new employees.

Unit20-c

I am encouraging all employees.
저는 모든 직원들에게 장려하고 있습니다.

I am encouraging all employees

설비 설명회에 모두 참석하도록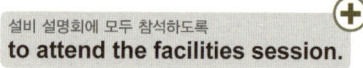
to attend the facilities session.

I am encouraging all employees to attend the facilities session

3월 30일에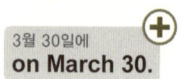
on March 30.

우리가 최근에 새로운 장소로 이전했기 때문에
Since we recently moved to a new location,

I am encouraging all employees to attend the facilities session on March 30.

Unit20-d Please consult my assistant.
제 비서에게 상의하세요.

Please consult my assistant,

Edwin Vargas에게 이 번호로
Edwin Vargas, at 323-555-0984.

Please consult my assistant, Edwin Vargas, at 323-555-0984

대안 방식들을 결정하기 위해
to make alternate arrangements.

설명회와 당신의 업무 스케줄에 충돌이 있다면,
Should any of the sessions conflict with your work schedule,

please consult my assistant, Edwin Vargas, at 323-555-0984 to make alternate arrangements.

Unit 17

To: Brad Franklin <brad@centech.com.>
     (이름)

From: John Lackey <jlackey@globemedia.com>
      (이름)

Subject: Junior Programmer Application
       신입 프로그래머 지원서

Hello Brad!
    (이름)

I can't believe it's been five years already since we
                        벌써 5년이 흘렀다

worked together. How are things with you?
우리가 함께 일한 이래로   어떻게 지내세요?

I am now a senior human resources recruiter at Globe-
               수석 인사담당자

media. Before coming here, I was human resources
(회사명)

manager at Pledge Alliance. My work at Globemedia is
            (회사명)

interesting. The company culture is a lot like it is where
흥미롭다   회사 문화   네가 있는 곳의 그것

you are.

I noticed your ad for a junior programmer in the New York Register newspaper. We have a young programmer here named Britta Forsberg who will complete her internship with us at the end of next month. I would love to be able to hire her full time, but Globemedia currently have no openings due to budget cuts and a hiring freeze. Ms. Forsberg is extremely talented. In the year she's been here, she has taken on increasing responsibilities, and she has become a person some senior programmers consult when they want a second opinion. I'd really like to see her find her work in a company that utilizes her skills.

If you would consider hiring Ms. Forsberg, let me know and I will have her forward her resume.

Best regards,

John

Unit 17

To: Brad Franklin <brad@centech.com.>

From: John Lackey <jlackey@globemedia.com>

Subject: Junior Programmer Application

Hello Brad!

I can't believe it's been five years already since we worked together. How are things with you?

I am now a senior human resources recruiter at Globemedia. Before coming here, I was human resources manager at Pledge Alliance. My work at Globemedia is interesting. The company culture is a lot like it is where you are.

I noticed your ad for a junior programmer in the New York Register newspaper. We have a young programmer here named Britta Forsberg who will complete her internship with us at the end of next month. I would love to be able to hire her full time, but Globemedia currently have no openings due to budget cuts and a hiring freeze. Ms. Forsberg is extremely talented. In the year she's been here, she has taken on increasing responsibilities, and she has become a person some senior programmers consult when they want a second opinion. I'd really like to see her find her work in a company that utilizes her skills.

If you would consider hiring Ms. Forsberg, let me know and I will have her forward her resume.

Best regards,

John

Unit 18

Dear Mr. Erickson;

All of us here at Andy's lumber wanted to let you, as one of our valued customers, know about our upcoming relocation and expansion. We will soon be moving to a bigger facility in Tacoma so that we may be closer to our suppliers. This will allow us to give you a better service and offer you a greater selection. Please refer to our newly updated website to get directions to the new site.

Our last day of business at our present location will be May 15th. We will open our doors in Tacoma on the 18th with a special reopening sale on tools and hardware items. The promotion lasts until the end of this month. Our new location will offer a regular 15% discount on all local lumber. Please be advised that we will be adding a huge new selection of imported lumber on June 1st. The Tacoma site will also have an expanded floor staff on hand to help you, and it will stay open one hour later every night. The facility will also have a bigger parking lot located right next to the sales area for convenient loading.

We look forward to seeing you again at our amazing new location.

Sincerely,

Unit 18

Dear Mr. Erickson;

All of us here at Andy's lumber wanted to let you, as one of our valued customers, know about our upcoming relocation and expansion. We will soon be moving to a bigger facility in Tacoma so that we may be closer to our suppliers. This will allow us to give you a better service and offer you a greater selection. Please refer to our newly updated website to get directions to the new site.

Our last day of business at our present location will be May 15th. We will open our doors in Tacoma on the 18th with a special reopening sale on tools and hardware items. The promotion lasts until the end of this month. Our new location will offer a regular 15% discount on all local lumber. Please be advised that we will be adding a huge new selection of imported lumber on June 1st. The Tacoma site will also have an expanded floor staff on hand to help you, and it will stay open one hour later every night. The facility will also have a bigger parking lot located right next to the sales area for convenient loading.

We look forward to seeing you again at our amazing new location.

Sincerely,

Unit 19

To: All Personnel

From: Andre Hoskins

Date: March 3

Subject: Information Sessions

To facilitate a successful start to the year, the human resources department will be holding the following information sessions this month as follows:

Session	Date	Time	Location
Safety	Mar. 8	2~4 P.M.	Conference Room A
Benefits	Mar. 11	9 A.M. ~ noon	Conference Room C
Computer Network	Mar. 22	10 A.M. ~ 1 P.M.	Conference Room H
Facilities	Mar. 30	10 A.M. ~ 1 P.M.	Conference Room I

Martin Rodriguez, my assistant, will be leading the safety and benefits sessions. Ellen Davis from the operations team will be leading the computer network and facilities sessions.

Please sign up in advance by sending an e-mail to Michael Santorello at misan@wide.com

Sincerely,

Andre Hoskins

Unit 19

To: All Personnel

From: Andre Hoskins

Date: March 3

Subject: Information Sessions

To facilitate a successful start to the year, the human resources department will be holding the following information sessions this month as follows:

Session	Date	Time	Location
Safety	Mar. 8	2~4 P.M.	Conference Room A
Benefits	Mar. 11	9 A.M. ~ noon	Conference Room C
Computer Network	Mar. 22	10 A.M. ~ 1 P.M.	Conference Room H
Facilities	Mar. 30	10 A.M. ~ 1 P.M.	Conference Room I

Martin Rodriguez, my assistant, will be leading the safety and benefits sessions. Ellen Davis from the operations team will be leading the computer network and facilities sessions.

Please sign up in advance by sending an e-mail to Michael Santorello at misan@wide.com

Sincerely,

Andre Hoskins

Unit 20

To: All personnel

From: Lohani Salzman, Vice President

Date: March 4

Subject: Information Sessions

The director of the human resources department recently sent you an e-mail that lists the various information sessions being offered this month. Please note that attendance at the March 8 session is mandatory for everyone, not just new employees.

Employees who work in the technical support department are required to attend the session on March 22.

Some important network training will be provided during that session, so attendees should be prepared to take notes.

Since we recently moved to a new location, I am encouraging all employees to attend the facilities session on March 30. Members of the building maintenance staff are required to attend this session as well.

Please register for the required sessions by March 5. Should any of the sessions conflict with your work schedule, please consult my assistant, Edwin Vargas, at 323-555-0984 to make alternate arrangements.

Unit 20

To: All personnel

From: Lohani Salzman, Vice President

Date: March 4

Subject: Information Sessions

The director of the human resources department recently sent you an e-mail that lists the various information sessions being offered this month. Please note that attendance at the March 8 session is mandatory for everyone, not just new employees.

Employees who work in the technical support department are required to attend the session on March 22.

Some important network training will be provided during that session, so attendees should be prepared to take notes.

Since we recently moved to a new location, I am encouraging all employees to attend the facilities session on March 30. Members of the building maintenance staff are required to attend this session as well.

Please register for the required sessions by March 5. Should any of the sessions conflict with your work schedule, please consult my assistant, Edwin Vargas, at 323-555-0984 to make alternate arrangements.

Unit 021-024
Preview

Unit21-a

We provide a guideline below.
우리는 아래의 지침을 제공합니다.

그 사건에 대응하여서 그리고 인정하여서
In response to that event and in recognition ⊕

we provide a guideline below.

In response to that event and in recognition

지역 사회에 절차의 공표가 도움되리라는 것을
that a declaration of procedures to the community would be helpful, ⊕

we provide a guideline below.

Unit21-b

Our goal is to provide.
우리의 목표는 제공하는 것입니다.

Our goal is to provide

가능한 한 안전한 환경을
as safe and secure an environment as possible. ⊕

140

Our goal is to provide as safe and secure an environment as possible

Camry Center에 있는 모두에게
for everyone at the Camry Center.

Unit21-c

You should know A and B.

당신들은 A와 B를 알아야 합니다.

You should know

신원 확인에 대한 지역사회의 반응이 좋았다는 것
that the response of the community to the ID checks has been excellent.

You should know that the response of the community to the ID checks has been excellent and

정중한 협조는 매우 감사 받고 있다는 것을
that the courteous cooperation is very much appreciated.

Unit 021-024
Preview

You should know that the response of the community to the ID checks has been excellent and that the courteous cooperation is very much appreciated

모든 보안 직원들에 의해서 ⊕
by all the security staff.

Unit22-a

Atlantic Printers will be presenting.
Atlantic Printers 는 진행할 것입니다.

Atlantic Printers will be presenting

매우 귀중한 세미나를 ⊕
an invaluable seminar.

Atlantic Printers will be presenting an invaluable seminar

영업과 마케팅 직종을 가진 사람들을 위한 ⊕
for those with jobs in sales and marketing.

12월 2일과 3일에,
On December 2 & 3,

Atlantic Printers will be presenting an invaluable seminar for those with jobs in sales and marketing.

Unit22-b

All employees will get reimbursed.
모든 직원들은 환급 받게 될 것입니다.

All employees

참석을 원하는
who wish to go

will get reimbursed.

All employees who wish to go will get reimbursed

멤버십과 등록, 점심, 교통에 대한 요금을
for their membership and registration, lunch and transportation fees.

Unit 021-024
Preview

Unit23-a

Please observe the following regulations.
다음의 규정을 준수해주십시오.

Please observe the following regulations

Brentwood Forest 공원 야영지에서
in Brentwood Forest Park Campgrounds: ⊕

공원에의 당신의 방문을 안전하고 즐겁게 만들기 위해서 ⊕
To make your visit to the park safe and enjoyable,

please observe the following regulations in Brentwood Forest Park Campgrounds:

To make your visit to the park safe and enjoyable,

그리고 공원 자원들의 보호를 위해 ⊕
and for the protection of the park resources,

please observe the following regulations in Brentwood Forest Park Campgrounds:

Unit23-b

Look for information.
정보를 찾으세요.

Look for information

먹이 주는 프로그램과 스케줄에 대한
on our feeding program and schedules.

Look for information on our feeding program and schedules

먹이 주기 장소 가까이 붙여진
posted near feeding sites.

만약 당신이 동물 먹이 주기에 참가하길 원하면,
If you want to participate in animal feeding,

look for information on our feeding program and schedules posted near feeding sites.

Unit 021-024
Preview

Unit23-c

Campers and other visitors are subject to expulsion.

야영객들과 다른 방문객들은 추방 될 수 있습니다.

Campers and other visitors are subject to expulsion

공원으로부터
from the park. ⊕

Campers and other visitors

공원 규정을 준수하지 않는
who fail to comply with park regulations ⊕

are subject to expulsion from the park.

Unit24-a

Students will learn.
학생들은 배울 것입니다.

Students will learn

프로그램들과 서비스들에 대해서
about the programs and services.

Students will learn about the programs and services

AU대학 캠퍼스에서 제공되는
offered campus wide at AU.

Students will learn about the programs and services offered campus wide at AU

학업 지원뿐 아니라
as well as the academic support.

Unit 021-024
Preview

Students will learn about the programs and services offered campus wide at AU as well as the academic support

대학 내에서 제공되는
offered within the college.

아침 설명회 동안에는
During the morning session,

students will learn about the programs and services offered campus wide at AU as well as the academic support offered within the college.

Unit24-b

Students will discuss and have the opportunity.

학생들은 의논할 것이고 기회를 가질 것입니다.

Students will discuss

전담 교수와 첫 학기 과정을
first semester courses with a faculty advisor

and have the opportunity.

Students will discuss first semester courses with a faculty advisor and have the opportunity

수업을 신청할
to register for classes.

예비 교육의 끝 무렵에는
Toward the end of orientation,

students will discuss first semester courses with a faculty advisor and have the opportunity to register for classes.

Unit 21

To: All staff
From: Mr. Martin Jackson, CEO
Date: April 5

Subject: Security Procedures

The employees and management at the Camry Center were very concerned about last week's bomb threat and subsequent evacuation. In response to that event and in recognition that a declaration of procedures to the community would be helpful, we provide a guideline below.

If a suspicious object is located:

(1) Under no circumstances should anyone move or touch a suspicious object or anything attached to it. Do not attempt to place the item in water.

(2) Report the location and an accurate description of the object to Security Hotline.

(3) If possible, open all doors and windows in the area to minimize primary damage from a blast and secondary damage from fragmentation.

Our goal is to provide as safe and secure an environment as possible for everyone at the Camry Center. As an added reminder, all employees will have their badges. You should know that the response of the community to the ID checks has been excellent and that the courteous cooperation is very much appreciated by all the security staff.

Unit 21

To: All staff

From: Mr. Martin Jackson, CEO

Date: April 5

Subject: Security Procedures

The employees and management at the Camry Center were very concerned about last week's bomb threat and subsequent evacuation. In response to that event and in recognition that a declaration of procedures to the community would be helpful, we provide a guideline below.

If a suspicious object is located:

(1) Under no circumstances should anyone move or touch a suspicious object or anything attached to it. Do not attempt to place the item in water.

(2) Report the location and an accurate description of the object to Security Hotline.

(3) If possible, open all doors and windows in the area to minimize primary damage from a blast and secondary damage from fragmentation.

Our goal is to provide as safe and secure an environment as possible for everyone at the Camry Center. As an added reminder, all employees will have their badges. You should know that the response of the community to the ID checks has been excellent and that the courteous cooperation is very much appreciated by all the security staff.

Unit 22

To: All employees
From: Donald Maxwell
Subject: Seminar / Date: May 17
Dear Colleagues,
I am happy to announce a future seminar that will benefit all those in attendance. On December 2 & 3, Atlantic Printers will be presenting an invaluable seminar for those with jobs in sales and marketing. It is needless to say that we are very proud that our co-worker, Fred Els, will be presenting. All employees who

wish to go will get reimbursed for their membership and registration, lunch and transportation fees.

Please come to my office and inform me after you have signed up if you would like to attend. If you can't make it to the seminar, I encourage you to simply sign up for an Atlantic Printers membership.

Sincerely,

Donald Maxwell

Date: December 2 ~ 3, 9 A.M. to 5 P.M.

Venue: Martel Convention Center, 2311 Finart Circle, Newark, New Jersey, U.S.A

Cost: $50 per day, or $95 for both days (for members)

$75 per day, or $140 for both days (for non-members)

(Complimentary lunch each day for all guests)

Membership: $115 per year (includes T-shirt and subscription to a weekly newsletter)

Unit 22

To: All employees

From: Donald Maxwell

Subject: Seminar / Date: May 17

Dear Colleagues,

I am happy to announce a future seminar that will benefit all those in attendance. On December 2 & 3, Atlantic Printers will be presenting an invaluable seminar for those with jobs in sales and marketing.

It is needless to say that we are very proud that our co-worker, Fred Els, will be presenting. All employees who wish to go will get reimbursed for their membership and registration, lunch and transportation fees.

Please come to my office and inform me after you have signed up if you would like to attend. If you can't make it to the seminar, I encourage you to simply sign up for an Atlantic Printers membership.

Sincerely,

Donald Maxwell

Date: December 2 ~ 3, 9 A.M. to 5 P.M.

Venue: Martel Convention Center, 2311 Finart Circle, Newark, New Jersey, U.S.A

Cost: $50 per day, or $95 for both days (for members)

$75 per day, or $140 for both days (for non-members)

(Complimentary lunch each day for all guests)

Membership: $115 per year (includes T-shirt and subscription to a weekly newsletter)

Unit 23

To make your visit to the park safe and enjoyable, and for the protection of the park resources, please observe the following regulations in Brentwood Forest Park Campgrounds:

- Camp at designated sites only in order to protect surrounding vegetation.
- Fires must be contained in park-provided grills. Extinguish all fires before leaving the area. Leave extinguished ashes in the grills.
- Wood within the park cannot be cut, collected or removed for any reason.

- Quiet hours are between 11P.M. and 6A.M. and are strictly observed.
- Keep pets on a leash at all times. Don't leave pets unattended.
- Secure trash day and night. Securely dispose of trash in dumpsters.
- Don't feed park animals including birds. If you want to participate in animal feeding, look for information on our feeding program and schedules posted near feeding sites.
- The following are prohibited in the campground: fire-arms, fireworks and weapons of any kind

This is your park. Protect it by reporting any violation of park regulations. Campers and other visitors who fail to comply with park regulations are subject to expulsion from the park. For further information, please contact the park visitor center at 762-555-5150. Enjoy your visit.

Unit 23

To make your visit to the park safe and enjoyable, and for the protection of the park resources, please observe the following regulations in Brentwood Forest Park Campgrounds:

- Camp at designated sites only in order to protect surrounding vegetation.
- Fires must be contained in park-provided grills. Extinguish all fires before leaving the area. Leave extinguished ashes in the grills.
- Wood within the park cannot be cut, collected or removed for any reason.

- Quiet hours are between 11P.M. and 6A.M. and are strictly observed.

- Keep pets on a leash at all times. Don't leave pets unattended.

- Secure trash day and night. Securely dispose of trash in dumpsters.

- Don't feed park animals including birds. If you want to participate in animal feeding, look for information on our feeding program and schedules posted near feeding sites.

- The following are prohibited in the campground: firearms, fireworks and weapons of any kind

This is your park. Protect it by reporting any violation of park regulations. Campers and other visitors who fail to comply with park regulations are subject to expulsion from the park. For further information, please contact the park visitor center at 762-555-5150. Enjoy your visit.

Unit 24

July 25
Dear students and parents,
All the faculty and staff, welcome to Southwest University.

This letter confirms your participation in the New Student Orientation. The orientation begins on the SU campus in Booth Hall. Please check in at the table labeled "College of Medicine" in the lobby of Booth Hall between 8:30 and 9 A.M.

During the orientation, you will meet with faculty and professional advisors, current SU students and other new students. During the morning session, students will learn about the programs and services offered campus wide at AU as well as the academic support offered within the college.

After the morning program, lunch is provided. Toward the end of orientation, students will discuss first semester courses with a faculty advisor and have the opportunity to register for classes. The orientation session will conclude at approximately 4 P.M.

Additional information is available on the SU homepage at www.su.edu. This site will provide you with all the information you will need, like general degree requirements. We are looking forward to meeting you at the New Student Orientation.

Sincerely,

Dr. Jamie Simpson, Director
College of Medicine

Unit 24

July 25

Dear students and parents,

All the faculty and staff, welcome to Southwest University.

This letter confirms your participation in the New Student Orientation. The orientation begins on the SU campus in Booth Hall. Please check in at the table labeled "College of Medicine" in the lobby of Booth Hall between 8:30 and 9 A.M.

During the orientation, you will meet with faculty and professional advisors, current SU students and other new students. During the morning session, students will learn about the programs and services offered campus wide at AU as well as the academic support offered within the college.

After the morning program, lunch is provided. Toward the end of orientation, students will discuss first semester courses with a faculty advisor and have the opportunity to register for classes. The orientation session will conclude at approximately 4 P.M.

Additional information is available on the SU homepage at www.su.edu. This site will provide you with all the information you will need, like general degree requirements. We are looking forward to meeting you at the New Student Orientation.

Sincerely,

Dr. Jamie Simpson, Director

College of Medicine

Unit 025-028
Preview

Unit25-a

I suggest.
저는 제안합니다.

두 달치 이자 부과를 피하기 위해서는
In order to avoid two months' worth of interest charges,

I suggest.

In order to avoid two months' worth of interest charges, I suggest

당신은 지불금을 송금해야 한다는 것을
that you remit payment.

In order to avoid two months' worth of interest charges, I suggest that you remit payment

가능한 빨리
as soon as possible.

Unit25-b

We will turn your account over.
우리는 당신의 계정을 넘길 것입니다.

We will turn your account over

미수금 처리 대행사에게
to a collection agency.

만약 우리가 지불금을 받지 못하면,
If we don't receive payment,

we will turn your account over to a collection agency.

If we don't receive payment

오늘로부터 세 달 후까지
after three months from today,

we will turn your account over to a collection agency.

Unit 025-028
Preview

Unit26-a

He will inspect the apartment.
그는 아파트를 점검할 것입니다.

He will inspect the apartment

보증하기 위해
to ensure.

He will inspect the apartment to ensure

원상태로 있는지
it is in the original condition.

He will inspect the apartment to ensure it is in the original condition

있던 그대로
as it was.

He will inspect the apartment to ensure it is in the original condition as it was

3년 전 당신이 이사 왔을 때
when you moved in three years ago.

Unit26-b

The $500 security deposit will be returned to you.
보증금 500달러를 당신에게 돌려 드릴 겁니다.

The $500 security deposit

당신이 이사 왔을 때 우리가 받았던
we received when you moved in

will be returned to you.

만약 아파트 점검이 통과되면,
If the apartment passes inspection,

the $500 security deposit we received when you moved in will be returned to you.

Unit26-c

You should return your apartment keys.
당신은 아파트 열쇠를 반납해야 합니다.

You should return your apartment keys

관리실에 있는 저희에게
to us in the management office.

Unit 025-028
Preview

You should return your apartment keys to us in the management office

당신의 건물 길 맞은 편에 있는
right across the street from your building.

이사 당일에,
On the day of your departure,

you should return your apartment keys to us in the management office right across the street from your building.

Unit27-a

We are extremely pleased and will certainly use.
우리는 매우 흡족하고 틀림 없이 이용할 것입니다.

We are extremely pleased and will certainly use

당신의 서비스를 미래에 다시
your services again in the future.

We are extremely pleased

훌륭한 작업물에
with the excellent work

and will certainly use your services again in the future.

We are extremely pleased with the excellent work

당신이 끝낸
you have done

and will certainly use your services again in the future.

Unit27-b **We need.**
우리는 필요합니다.

We need

당신의 도움을
your assistance.

We need your assistance

몇 가지 다른 문제에 관해
with a couple of other matters.

Unit 025-028
Preview

We need your assistance with a couple of other matters

이 과제를 완료하기 위해서
to complete this assignment.

Unit27-c

Please e-mail me.
저에게 이메일로 보내주세요.

Please e-mail me

그 정보를 다시
with that information again.

Please e-mail me with that information again

가능한 빨리
as soon as possible.

Please e-mail me with that information again as soon as possible

우리가 당신에게 지체 없이 돈을 지불할 수 있도록
so that we can pay you promptly.

Unit28-a

I don't believe.
저는 생각하지 않습니다.

I don't believe

이 변화들이 충분하게 고려 되고 있는 것이라고
that these changes are being thought properly.

비록 제가 그 바람을 이해하긴 하지만,
Although I understand the wish,

I don't believe that these changes are being thought properly.

Although I understand the wish

사무실에서 에너지를 절약하려는
to save energy in the offices,

I don't believe that these changes are being thought properly.

Unit 025-028
Preview

Unit28-b

There is no problem, but I will have to say.
문제가 없지만 제가 말을 해야겠습니다.

There is no problem

전자 제품을 교체하는 데에는
with replacing electrical devices,

but I will have to say.

There is no problem with replacing electrical devices

건전지 제품들로
with battery-operated ones,

but I will have to say.

There is no problem with replacing electrical devices with battery-operated ones, but I will have to say

저는 그 생각에 반대한다고
that I'm against the idea.

There is no problem with replacing electrical devices with battery-operated ones, but I will have to say that I'm against the idea

와트 수가 낮은 전구들을 사용하는
of using lower wattage bulbs.

Unit28-c

I am afraid.
저는 염려스럽습니다.

I am afraid

와트 수가 낮은 전구는 우리의 업무를 악화시키고 눈의 피로를 야기할 수 있다는 것이
that the lower wattage will impair our work and could cause eyestrain.

I am afraid that the lower wattage,

적은 빛을 내는 것을 의미하는
which means less light,

will impair our work and could cause eyestrain.

Unit 25

Name: Todd Jones / Account number: 289-0047
　　　이름　　　　　　　　　계정 번호

Service date: March 15 / Balance due: $650.00
　　　　　　　　　　　　　　지불할 금액

Due date: April 15
지불 기한

Our customer service department is available Monday
　　　고객 서비스 부서　　　　　　　　이용 가능한

to Friday 8:00 A.M. ~ 5:30 P.M. / 626-441-4489
월요일부터 금요일까지

Send payment by check or money order to:
　지불액　　　수표　　　우편환

Express Auto Repair 7902 9th Ave, Atlanta, GA
　　(회사명)

Past due accounts will be charged 10% interest per month.
연체시　　계좌　　청구 되어질 것이다　　　이자

Todd Jones, 1628 5th Ave. Seattle, WA
(이름)

Dear Mr. Jones,

It has come to our attention that you have an outstanding bill with our company. You received repairs on your 2005 sedan on 3/15 and we were expecting payment by 4/15. It is now 5/15.

As stated on the bill, we must charge overdue accounts 10% interest each month that payment is overdue. On the 15th, our service department replaced the spark plugs and repaired the radiator on your vehicle. If these repairs were unsatisfactory, pleases let us know. In order to avoid two months' worth of interest charges, I suggest that you remit payment as soon as possible. If we don't receive payment after three months from today, we will turn your account over to a collection agency. Collection agencies tend to charge much higher interest rates on overdue accounts.

Please take care of the matter as soon as possible.

Janice Rey, Billing Department

Unit 25

Name: Todd Jones / Account number: 289-0047

Service date: March 15 / Balance due: $650.00

Due date: April 15

Our customer service department is available Monday to Friday 8:00 A.M. ~ 5:30 P.M. / 626-441-4489

Send payment by check or money order to:

Express Auto Repair 7902 9th Ave, Atlanta, GA

Past due accounts will be charged 10% interest per month.

Todd Jones, 1628 5th Ave. Seattle, WA

Dear Mr. Jones,

It has come to our attention that you have an outstanding bill with our company. You received repairs on your 2005 sedan on 3/15 and we were expecting payment by 4/15. It is now 5/15.

As stated on the bill, we must charge overdue accounts 10% interest each month that payment is overdue. On the 15th, our service department replaced the spark plugs and repaired the radiator on your vehicle. If these repairs were unsatisfactory, pleases let us know. In order to avoid two months' worth of interest charges, I suggest that you remit payment as soon as possible. If we don't receive payment after three months from today, we will turn your account over to a collection agency. Collection agencies tend to charge much higher interest rates on overdue accounts.

Please take care of the matter as soon as possible.

Janice Rey, Billing Department

Unit 26

BC Building Management, 7575 Walnut Place
　　　(회사명)

Vancouver, British Columbia T5J 1N7 / June 10
　(도시명)　　　　　(주명)

Mr. Ken Griffey, 6550 Walnut Place, Apt. 10B, Vancou-
　　(이름)

ver, British Columbia T5J 1N7

Dear Mr. Griffey

We appreciate your early notification that your intent to
　　감사하다　　　　이른 통보　　　　　　　　의도

move out on June 30. As that date approaches, we would
이사 나가다　　　　　　그 날짜가 다가옴에 따라

like to inform you of some important procedures.
　　　알리다　　　　　몇 가지 중요한 절차

The maintenance supervisor, Mr. Stevenson, will visit
　　건물유지 관리자　　　　동격　　　(이름)

your apartment on June 29. On that date, he will inspect
　　　　　　　　　　　　　　그날　　　　점검할 것이다

the apartment to ensure it is in the original condition as
　　　　　　　보증하기 위해　　　　　　원상태

it was when you moved in three years ago. If the apart-
있던대로　　　3년 전 당신이 이사 왔을 때

ment passes inspection, the $500 security deposit we received when you moved in will be returned to you. However, in the event that the apartment does not pass inspection, one-half of the deposit will be returned. When removing your belongings from the apartment, please refrain from using the main elevators by the mail room. They are not large enough to accommodate furniture and other bulky items. Instead, please use the service elevator located near the exit at the back of the building. On the day of your departure, you should return your apartment keys to us in the management office right across the street from your building. Please note, you will no longer have access to your apartment after the keys are returned. So, make certain to remove all your belongings from the apartment before returning the key. If you have any further questions or inquiries, feel free to contact me at 780-555-0145.
Sincerely, Saichand Kapoor, Property Manager

Unit 26

BC Building Management, 7575 Walnut Place

Vancouver, British Columbia T5J 1N7 / June 10

Mr. Ken Griffey, 6550 Walnut Place, Apt. 10B, Vancouver, British Columbia T5J 1N7

Dear Mr. Griffey

We appreciate your early notification that your intent to move out on June 30. As that date approaches, we would like to inform you of some important procedures.

The maintenance supervisor, Mr. Stevenson, will visit your apartment on June 29. On that date, he will inspect the apartment to ensure it is in the original condition as it was when you moved in three years ago. If the apartment passes inspection, the $500 security deposit we received when you moved in will be returned to you. However, in the event that the apartment does not pass inspection, one-half of the deposit will be returned.

When removing your belongings from the apartment, please refrain from using the main elevators by the mail room. They are not large enough to accommodate furniture and other bulky items. Instead, please use the service elevator located near the exit at the back of the building. On the day of your departure, you should return your apartment keys to us in the management office right across the street from your building. Please note you will no longer have access to your apartment after the keys are returned. So, make certain to remove all your belongings from the apartment before returning the key. If you have any further questions or inquiries, feel free to contact me at 780-555-0145.

Sincerely, Saichand Kapoor, Property Manager

Unit 27

Dear Ms. Safina,

We received your translation of the strategy materials last week. We are extremely pleased with the excellent work you have done and will certainly use your services again in the future. We need your assistance with a couple of other matters to complete this assignment. First, as we need the original materials for our files, would you please return those to us? Secondly, you had

asked for your fee to be deposited into your bank account. Unfortunately, I seem to have deleted the e-mail message that had your account number. Please e-mail me with that information again as soon as possible so that we can pay you promptly.
Thank you very much.

Best regards,

Raul Gonzales

Unit 27

Dear Ms. Safina,

We received your translation of the strategy materials last week. We are extremely pleased with the excellent work you have done and will certainly use your services again in the future. We need your assistance with a couple of other matters to complete this assignment.

First, as we need the original materials for our files, would you please return those to us? Secondly, you had asked for your fee to be deposited into your bank account. Unfortunately, I seem to have deleted the e-mail message that had your account number. Please e-mail me with that information again as soon as possible so that we can pay you promptly.

Thank you very much.

Best regards,

Raul Gonzales

Unit 28

Mr. Messi,

Although I understand the wish to save energy in the offices, I don't believe that these changes are being thought properly. There is no problem with replacing electrical devices with battery-operated ones, but I will have to say that I'm against the idea of using lower wattage bulbs. As you are well aware, as architects, we spend a whole day hunched over blueprints and our work is very intricate and detailed. I am afraid that the lower wattage, which means less light, will impair our work and could cause eyestrain. What are your thoughts on this?

Frank Lampard

Unit 28

Mr. Messi,

Although I understand the wish to save energy in the offices, I don't believe that these changes are being thought properly. There is no problem with replacing electrical devices with battery-operated ones, but I will have to say that I'm against the idea of using lower wattage bulbs. As you are well aware, as architects, we spend a whole day hunched over blueprints and our work is very intricate and detailed. I am afraid that the lower wattage, which means less light, will impair our work and could cause eyestrain. What are your thoughts on this?

Frank Lampard

Unit 029-032
Preview

Unit29-a

"Casual Days" are becoming very popular.
"캐주얼 입는 날"은 매우 인기 있어 지고 있다.

"Casual Days",

직원들이 덜 격식 있게 입도록 권장되는
on which employees are encouraged to dress less formally,

are becoming very popular.

"Casual Days", on which employees are encouraged to dress less formally

일반적인 정장과 넥타이로 입는 것보다
than in the standard suit and tie,

are becoming very popular.

Unit29-b

I think.
저는 생각합니다.

I think

경영진들은 스스로를 차별화할 수 있다고
executives can set themselves apart.

I think executives can set themselves apart

품위 있는 장신구들로
with status accessories.

I think executives can set themselves apart with status accessories

알맞은 시계, 신발, 안경과 펜과 같은
like the right watch, shoes, glasses, and pen.

Unit30-a **We have reviewed and regret.**
우리는 검토하였고 유감스럽습니다.

We have reviewed

당신 집에 대한 2순위 담보 대출에 관한 신청서를
your application for a second mortgage on your home

and reget.

We have reviewed your application for a second mortgage on your home and regret

당신에게 알리는 것이
to inform you.

Unit 029-032
Preview

We have reviewed your application for a second mortgage on your home and regret to inform you

당신에게 제공할 수 없을 것이라는 것을
that we will not be able to provide you.

We have reviewed your application for a second mortgage on your home and regret to inform you that we will not be able to provide you

어떠한 재정 지원도
with any financial assistance.

Unit30-b
You are currently behind and are using.

당신은 현재 넘어섰고 사용하고 있습니다.

You are currently behind

당신의 기존의 보증 대출 지급을
on your existing mortgage payments

and are using.

You are currently behind on your existing mortgage payments and are using

높은 이자의 신용 카드들을
high-interest credit cards.

우리의 신용 평가에 따르면,
According to our credit check,

you are currently behind on your existing mortgage payments and are using high-interest credit cards.

Unit30-c

Your bank reference has indicated.
당신 은행 신용조회는 알려줍니다.

Your bank reference has indicated

몇몇 문제점과 자본의 부족을
some issues and lack of funds.

Unit 029-032
Preview

Your bank reference has indicated some issues

with bounded checks (부도수표들의)

and lack of funds.

Your bank reference has indicated some issues with bounced checks and lack of funds

in your account. (당신의 계좌에 있는)

Unit31-a We host Victoria Café night.
우리는 Victoria 카페의 밤을 주최합니다.

We host Victoria Café night,

which features entertainment by local musicians. (지역 음악가들에 의한 여흥거리를 특색으로 하는)

196

We host Victoria Café night, which features entertainment by local musicians

무료 커피와 디저트들과
and free coffee and desserts.

We host Victoria Café night, which features entertainment by local musicians and free coffee and desserts

오후 8시부터 10시까지
from 8 to 10 p.m.

매달 첫 번째 금요일에,
On the first Friday of each month,

we host Victoria Café night, which features entertainment by local musicians and free coffee and desserts from 8 to 10 p.m.

Unit 029–032
Preview

Unit31-b

Please e-mail.
이메일로 보내주세요.

Please e-mail

디지털 사진들을
digital photographs.

Please e-mail digital photographs

대표적인 견본들의
of representative samples.

Please e-mail digital photographs of representative samples

당신 작품들의
of your work.

만약 당신이 Victoria Island 시장 가족으로 함께하기를 원하면,
If you would like to join Victoria Island marketplace family,

please e-mail digital photographs of representative samples of your work.

Unit32-a

Our concierge service would be delighted.
우리 안내 서비스는 기쁠 것입니다.

Our concierge service would be delighted

관광 활동을 추천해 드리는 것에
to recommend tourist activities.

Our concierge service would be delighted to recommend tourist activities

이 멋진 섬에서
in this gorgeous island.

Our concierge service would be delighted to recommend tourist activities in this gorgeous island

그리고 어떤 식당에서든 당신에게 테이블을 예약해 드리는 것에
and book you a table at any restaurant.

Unit 029-032
Preview

만약 당신이 발리를 탐사하길 원한다면,
If you would like to explore Bali,

our concierge service would be delighted to recommend tourist activities in this gorgeous island and book you a table at any restaurant.

Unit32-b

Would you take the time?
시간을 할애해 주시겠어요?

Would you take the time

고객 만족도 조사를 작성하는 데에
to fill in a customer satisfaction survey?

Would you take the time to fill in a customer satisfaction survey

각 방과 웹사이트에서 이용할 수 있는
that is available in each room and on our website?

머무시고 난 후에,
After your stay,

would you take the time to fill in a customer satisfaction survey that is available in each room and on our website?

Unit 29

Dear Marilyn

It's "Casual Day" in our office every Friday. Almost all the men wear the same thin-pleated khakis, a new blazer, and a white oxford shirt. I think I should wear something **different** to distinguish myself from everyone else.
What should I wear?
Thank you in advance for your quick reply.

Sincerely,
CEO in London

Dear CEO:

"Casual Days", on which employees are encouraged to dress less formally than in the standard suit and tie, are becoming very popular. I took your question to Tucker Alexander, fashion editor of the popular men's magazine, Men. He said, "Bottom line: the president should always look elegant. He could wear a cashmere sport jacket with flannel gabardine trousers and a knit polo shirt, or a sporty matching shirt-and-tie combination." Personally, I think executives can set themselves apart with status accessories, like the right watch, shoes, glasses, and pen.

Unit 29

Dear Marilyn

It's "Casual Day" in our office every Friday. Almost all the men wear the same thin-pleated khakis, a new blazer, and a white oxford shirt. I think I should wear something different to distinguish myself from everyone else.

What should I wear?

Thank you in advance for your quick reply.

Sincerely,

CEO in London

Dear CEO:

"Casual Days", on which employees are encouraged to dress less formally than in the standard suit and tie, are becoming very popular. I took your question to Tucker Alexander, fashion editor of the popular men's magazine, Men. He said, "Bottom line: the president should always look elegant. He could wear a cashmere sport jacket with flannel gabardine trousers and a knit polo shirt, or a sporty matching shirt-and-tie combination." Personally, I think executives can set themselves apart with status accessories, like the right watch, shoes, glasses, and pen.

Unit 30

Mrs. Danilova
(이름)

315 South Virgil, Los Angeles

Dear Mrs. Danilova

We have reviewed your application for a second mortgage on your home and regret to inform you that we will not be able to provide you with any financial assistance. According to our credit check, you are currently behind on your existing mortgage payments and are using high-interest credit cards.

In addition, your bank reference has indicated some issues with bounced checks and lack of funds in your account.

It is our policy to deny loans to anyone with a high-risk profile. If you require any further assistance, please contact our Risk Management department and they will be pleased to help you.

Sincerely, Simon Morgan

Financial Assessment Director

Unit 30

Mrs. Danilova

315 South Virgil, Los Angeles

Dear Mrs. Danilova

We have reviewed your application for a second mortgage on your home and regret to inform you that we will not be able to provide you with any financial assistance. According to our credit check, you are currently behind on your existing mortgage payments and are using high-interest credit cards.

In addition, your bank reference has indicated some issues with bounced checks and lack of funds in your account.

It is our policy to deny loans to anyone with a high-risk profile. If you require any further assistance, please contact our Risk Management department and they will be pleased to help you.

Sincerely, Simon Morgan

Financial Assessment Director

Unit 31

Dear Ms. Yuki,
(이름)

Thank you for your interest in Victoria Marketplace. For
관심   빅토리아 시장(시장명)

more than 10 years, we have been selling arts and crafts
10년 이상 동안   판매 해 오고있다   공예품들

made exclusively by Victoria Island artisans. Paintings,
        오로지   빅토리아 섬(지역명)   장인들   그림

jewelry, clothing, and holiday decorations are among
보석   의류   기념일 장식품들

the items offered for sale. We only accept the items that
항목 중에 판매 되어지는   받아 들인다

are made by hand, and we obtain them directly from
    수공품의   구한다   곧장

their creators; we do not accept any imported items.
    작가들   수입품

On the first Friday of each month, we host Victoria Café
매달 첫번째 금요일에   추최하다   파티 이름

night, which features entertainment by local musicians and free coffee and desserts from 8 to 10 p.m. Café Night is highly publicized and typically attracts up to 300 tourists and area residents.

If you would like to join Victoria Island marketplace family, please e-mail digital photographs of representative samples of your work. Also let us know of any art schools you have attended. We will contact you within one week with further instructions.

Best regards,

Unit 31

Dear Ms. Yuki,

Thank you for your interest in Victoria Marketplace. For more than 10 years, we have been selling arts and crafts made exclusively by Victoria Island artisans. Paintings, jewelry, clothing, and holiday decorations are among the items offered for sale. We only accept the items that are made by hand, and we obtain them directly from their creators; we do not accept any imported items.

On the first Friday of each month, we host Victoria Café

night, which features entertainment by local musicians and free coffee and desserts from 8 to 10 p.m. Café Night is highly publicized and typically attracts up to 300 tourists and area residents.

If you would like to join Victoria Island marketplace family, please e-mail digital photographs of representative samples of your work. Also let us know of any art schools you have attended. We will contact you within one week with further instructions.

Best regards,

Unit 32

To: Patrick Stewart
　　　(이름)
From: Front desk
　　　안내 데스크
Subject: Reservation confirmation
　　　　예약 확인
Date: March 12

Thank you for choosing Banyan tree Hotel in Bali. This
　　　　　　　　　　　　반얀트리(호텔명)
e-mail is to confirm your reservation for April 10~15.
　　　　확인 하기 위해
While you stay with us, please try our award-winning
　당신이 우리와 머무는 동안　　　　　　　　　상을 받은
restaurant featuring the culinary talents of Chef Nicolas
　　　　　특징으로 삼다　　요리의 재능
Wilson, and our poolside café. If you would like to ex-
(이름)　　　　　　풀장 가
plore Bali, our concierge service would be delighted to
탐사하길　　　　안내 서비스　　　　　　기쁠 것이다
recommend tourist activities in this gorgeous island and
추천하기에　　관광 활동　　　　　아주 멋진 섬

book you a table at any restaurant.

After your stay, would you take the time to fill in a customer satisfaction survey that is available in each room and on our website? We will send you a voucher for one free night at any of our hotel locations, including Sydney and Bangkok. For a complete listing of locations and information about our grand opening in Kuala Lumpur, please visit our website.

If you have any questions or inquiries, please contact us at 62 3 555 0202.

The Banyan tree Hotel

Unit 32

To: Patrick Stewart

From: Front desk

Subject: Reservation confirmation

Date: March 12

Thank you for choosing Banyan tree Hotel in Bali. This e-mail is to confirm your reservation for April 10~15.

While you stay with us, please try our award-winning restaurant featuring the culinary talents of Chef Nicolas Wilson, and our poolside café. If you would like to explore Bali, our concierge service would be delighted to recommend tourist activities in this gorgeous island and book you a table at any restaurant.

After your stay, would you take the time to fill in a customer satisfaction survey that is available in each room and on our website? We will send you a voucher for one free night at any of our hotel locations, including Sydney and Bangkok. For a complete listing of locations and information about our grand opening in Kuala Lumpur, please visit our website.

If you have any questions or inquiries, please contact us at 62 3 555 0202.

The Banyan tree Hotel

Unit 033-036
Preview

Unit33-a

This was my first visit.
저의 첫 번째 방문이었습니다.

This was my first visit

발리에 있는 당신의 호텔로는
to your hotel in Bali.

비록 제가 머물렀었지만,
Although I have stayed,

this was my first visit to your hotel in Bali.

Although I have stayed

다른 지역의 그 호텔에서
at the hotel's other locations,

this was my first visit to your hotel in Bali.

Although I have stayed at the hotel's other locations

출장 가있는 동안에
while on business,

this was my first visit to your hotel in Bali.

Unit33-b

I would like to ask.
질문하고 싶습니다.

I would like to ask

쿠폰이 유효한지 그렇지 않은지
if the coupon will be valid.

I would like to ask if the coupon will be valid

나중에 생기는 지점에서도
at your future location.

쿠폰에 관하여,
As for my voucher,

I would like to ask if the coupon will be valid at your future location.

Unit 033-036
Preview

Unit33-c

Your website indicates, and I have to go.
당신의 웹사이트는 명시하고 있으며, 저는 가야 합니다.

Your website indicates

1월에 개점하기로 예정되어있다고
that the grand opening is scheduled for January,

and I have to go.

Your website indicates that the grand opening is scheduled for January, and I have to go

거기에서 있는 회의에
to a conference there.

Your website indicates that the grand opening is scheduled for January, and I have to go to a conference there

2월에
in February.

Unit34-a

I'm leaving and am hoping.
저는 떠날 것이며 또한 바라고 있습니다.

I'm leaving

다음 주에 가나로 출장을
on a business trip to Ghana next week

and am hoping.

I'm leaving on a business trip to Ghana next week and am hoping

당신이 저에게 보편적인 충고를 제공해주기를
you can offer me some general advice.

I'm leaving on a business trip to Ghana next week and am hoping you can offer me some general advice

그곳에서의 비즈니스를 하는 것에 대해서
about doing business there.

Unit 033-036
Preview

Unit34-b

I'm especially eager.
저는 특히 열망합니다.

I'm especially eager

그것이 성공하기를
for it to be a success.

이것은 저의 첫 번째 출장이기 때문에,
Since this is the first trip,

I'm especially eager for it to be a success.

Since this is the first trip

영업 과장으로써 맡은
I have taken as the sales manager,

I'm especially eager for it to be a success.

Unit35-a

This will allow you.
이것은 당신에게 가능하게 할 것이다.

This will allow you

관여하는 것을
to engage.

222

This will allow you to engage

즐거운 대화에
in some enjoyable discussions.

This will allow you to engage in some enjoyable discussions

당신의 거래처와의
with your business contacts.

Unit35-b

Figure out.
정하세요.

Figure out

사전에 당신의 상사와
with your supervisor beforehand.

Figure out with your supervisor beforehand

어떤 종류의 타협들을 당신이 이루려고 하는지
what kinds of compromises you should be willing to make.

Unit 033-036
Preview

Unit35-c

The negotiations are going well.
협상은 잘 되고 있습니다.

The negotiations

스위스 동료들과 함께
with our Swiss colleagues ⊕

are going well.

The negotiations with our Swiss colleagues are going well

지금까지 ⊕
so far.

The negotiations with our Swiss colleagues are going well so far,

하지만 우리는 협상을 한창 진행 중입니다 ⊕
but we're right in the middle of them.

The negotiations with our Swiss colleagues are going well so far, but we're right in the middle of them,

아직 확신할 수 없습니다.
so I'm not counting on anything yet.

Unit36-a

I came to know you.
저는 당신을 알게 되었습니다.

I came to know you

Alfonso Soriano라는 저의 동료를 통해서
through my colleague, Alfonso Soriano.

I came to know you through my colleague, Alfonso Soriano,

당신이 굉장한 일을 했다고 말한
who said you did an awesome job.

I came to know you through my colleague, Alfonso Soriano, who said you did an awesome job

부서 저녁 행사에서
with his department's dinner party.

Unit 033-036
Preview

I came to know you through my colleague, Alfonso Soriano, who said you did an awesome job with his department's dinner party

지난 달에
last month.

Unit36-b | I was wondering.
저는 궁금했습니다.

당신의 행사 음식 메뉴를 온라인에서 확인했는데
I checked your catering menu online and

I was wondering.

I checked your catering menu online and I was wondering

가능 할지
if it would be possible.

I checked your catering menu online and I was wondering if it would be possible

메뉴 항목들을 바꾸는 것이
to make changed menu items.

Unit36-c

Could we hire?
우리가 고용할 수 있을까요?

Could we hire

당신의 식당에서 서버를
a server from your restaurant?

Could we hire a server from your restaurant

도와줄
to help?

Could we hire a server from your restaurant to help

오전 11시 30분부터 오후 2시쯤까지
from 11:30 a.m. to around 2 p.m.?

Unit 33

Name: Patrick Stewart

Comments and Questions

Although I have stayed at the hotel's other locations while on business, this was my first visit to your hotel in Bali. For the most part, I am satisfied with the services. However, I was wrongly charged. This particular time, I was charged two times for movies that I didn't watch. In fact, I did not watch movies at all during my stay; I only watched the free TV. When I pointed this out to the desk clerk, the situation was resolved right away. I was very impressed with the hospitality of staff.

As for my voucher, I would like to ask if the coupon will be valid at your future location. Your website indicates that the grand opening is scheduled for January, and I have to go to a conference there in February.

Unit 33

Name: Patrick Stewart

Comments and Questions

Although I have stayed at the hotel's other locations while on business, this was my first visit to your hotel in Bali. For the most part, I am satisfied with the services. However, I was wrongly charged. This particular time, I was charged two times for movies that I didn't watch. In fact, I did not watch movies at all during my stay; I only watched the free TV. When I pointed this out to the desk clerk, the situation was resolved right away. I was very impressed with the hospitality of staff.

As for my voucher, I would like to ask if the coupon will be valid at your future location. Your website indicates that the grand opening is scheduled for January, and I have to go to a conference there in February.

Unit 34

To: Ryan Federer <ryan@itotrading.com>
   (이름)

From: Erick Ferra <erick@ itotrading.com>
   이름

Date: March 4

Subject: Recommendations
   권고

Ryan,

Your assistant told me you don't get back until the week
   조수
after next, so I hope you don't mind my e-mailing you.
다음 다음주
I'm leaving on a business trip to Ghana next week and
   출장   (국가명)
am hoping you can offer me some general advice about
   제공할 수 있다   보편적인 충고

doing business there. I know a lot of your work takes you throughout Africa; therefore, any guidance you can offer will be a great help. Since this is the first trip I have taken as the sales manager, I'm especially eager for it to be a success.

Good luck with your business discussions. I trust they're doing as well as you had hoped.

Take care, and see you soon.

Erick

Unit 34

To: Ryan Federer <ryan@itotrading.com>

From: Erick Ferra <erick@ itotrading.com>

Date: March 4

Subject: Recommendations

Ryan,

Your assistant told me you don't get back until the week after next, so I hope you don't mind my e-mailing you. I'm leaving on a business trip to Ghana next week and am hoping you can offer me some general advice about doing business there. I know a lot of your work takes you throughout Africa; therefore, any guidance you can offer will be a great help. Since this is the first trip I have taken as the sales manager, I'm especially eager for it to be a success.

Good luck with your business discussions. I trust they're doing as well as you had hoped.

Take care, and see you soon.

Erick

Unit 35

To: Erick Ferra <erick@itotrading.com>

From: Ryan Federer <ryan@itotrading.com>

Date: March 5

Subject: Re: Recommendations

Erick,

I'm happy to offer any assistance I can. I assume you are planning to do a little research on Ghana before you go. When you arrive, you should try to visit a few places of cultural and historical interest. This will allow you to engage in some enjoyable discussions with your business contacts.

Traffic can be a big problem in the capital city, Accra;

you should take this into consideration as it is important to arrive on time for appointments. Once your negotiations begin, be prepared to enter into them with a spirit of give-and-take. Perhaps figure out with your supervisor beforehand what kinds of compromises you should be willing to make.
The negotiations with our Swiss colleagues are going well so far, but we're right in the middle of them, so I'm not counting on anything yet. We still have a lot of work to do before the deal is complete.
Have a great trip. See you at the next staff meeting.

Ryan

Unit 35

To: Erick Ferra <erick@itotrading.com>

From: Ryan Federer <ryan@itotrading.com>

Date: March 5

Subject: Re: Recommendations

Erick,

I'm happy to offer any assistance I can. I assume you are planning to do a little research on Ghana before you go. When you arrive, you should try to visit a few places of cultural and historical interest. This will allow you to engage in some enjoyable discussions with your business contacts.

Traffic can be a big problem in the capital city, Accra;

you should take this into consideration as it is important to arrive on time for appointments. Once your negotiations begin, be prepared to enter into them with a spirit of give-and-take. Perhaps figure out with your supervisor beforehand what kinds of compromises you should be willing to make.

The negotiations with our Swiss colleagues are going well so far, but we're right in the middle of them, so I'm not counting on anything yet. We still have a lot of work to do before the deal is complete.

Have a great trip. See you at the next staff meeting.

Ryan

Unit 36

Subject: Catering order

Date: December 10

Dear Rossi,

I came to know you through my colleague, Alfonso Soriano, who said you did an awesome job with his department's dinner party last month. He highly recommended you for my department's upcoming luncheon on Friday, December 18. About 50 people are expected to attend. Before I place an order for this event, I have a few questions to be answered.

I checked your catering menu online and I was wondering if it would be possible to make changed menu items.

For example, I'd like to order Lasagna Classic but without the meat. Could the lasagna be made with spinach and mushrooms instead? The thing is there are quite a few vegetarians in my department. I also wondered if there is a separate charge for delivery. Finally, could we hire a server from your restaurant to help from 11:30 a.m. to around 2 p.m.?

Please call me at 312-555-8282 at your earliest convenience to answer these questions. I'll give you details of the order and my credit card number at that time.

Thank you

Jay Letterman

Unit 36

Subject: Catering order

Date: December 10

Dear Rossi,

I came to know you through my colleague, Alfonso Soriano, who said you did an awesome job with his department's dinner party last month. He highly recommended you for my department's upcoming luncheon on Friday, December 18. About 50 people are expected to attend. Before I place an order for this event, I have a few questions to be answered.

I checked your catering menu online and I was wondering if it would be possible to make changed menu items.

For example, I'd like to order Lasagna Classic but without the meat. Could the lasagna be made with spinach and mushrooms instead? The thing is there are quite a few vegetarians in my department. I also wondered if there is a separate charge for delivery. Finally, could we hire a server from your restaurant to help from 11:30 a.m. to around 2 p.m.?

Please call me at 312-555-8282 at your earliest convenience to answer these questions. I'll give you details of the order and my credit card number at that time.

Thank you

Jay Letterman

Unit 037-040
Preview

Unit37-a

I was still left.
저는 방치됐었습니다.

I was still left

거의 일주일 동안 난방 없이
without heat for almost a week.

제가 인정하지만,
While I acknowledge,

I was still left without heat for almost a week.

While I acknowledge

Ms. Sandra and Mr. Wright가 모든 것을 다했다는 것을
that Ms. Sandra and Mr. Wright did everything,

I was still left without heat for almost a week.

While I acknowledge that Ms. Sandra and Mr. Wright did everything

문제를 고치기 위해 그들이 할 수 있었던 ⊕
they could to fix the problem,

I was still left without heat for almost a week.

While I acknowledge that Ms. Sandra and Mr. Wright did everything they could to fix the problem

가능한 한 빨리 ⊕
as quickly as possible,

I was still left without heat for almost a week.

Unit 037-040
Preview

Unit37-b
I am expecting.
저는 예상합니다.

I am expecting

제 전기세가
my electric bill.

I am expecting my electric bill

거의 두 배가 될 것으로
to be nearly double.

I am expecting my electric bill to be nearly double

약 120달러쯤 나오는 보통의 요금의
the usual fee of around $120.

Unit38-a
I am very sorry to hear.
듣게 되어서 유감입니다.

I am very sorry to hear

난방 장치가 고장 상태였다는 것을
that the heating system was out of commission.

I am very sorry to hear that the heating system

당신 아파트에 있는
in your apartment

was out of commission.

I am very sorry to hear that the heating system in your apartment was out of commission

그렇게 길어진 기간 동안
for such an extended period of time.

Unit38-b

I will be mailing you.
당신에게 송금할 것입니다.

I will be mailing you

상환 금액 수표를
a reimbursement check.

I will be mailing you a reimbursement check

동액의
in the amount.

Unit 037-040
Preview

I will be mailing you a reimbursement check in the amount

당신이 요청한
that you requested.

Unit39-a

The Sunshine Hotel is pleased.
Sunshine 호텔은 기쁩니다.

The Sunshine Hotel is pleased

당신이 며칠 밤을 저희 호텔에서 머무를 것을 고려하고 있다는 것이
that you are considering coming to stay with us for a few nights.

The Sunshine Hotel is pleased that you are considering coming to stay with us for a few nights

그리고 이 안내 책자를 만들었습니다.
and we have designed this brochure.

The Sunshine Hotel is pleased that you are considering coming to stay with us for a few nights and we have designed this brochure

당신을 돕기 위해서
to assist you.

The Sunshine Hotel is pleased that you are considering coming to stay with us for a few nights and we have designed this brochure to assist you

객실 예약 과정에서
in the room reservation process.

The Sunshine Hotel is pleased that you are considering coming to stay with us for a few nights and we have designed this brochure to assist you in the room reservation process

당신의 체류를 보다 간편하게 만들기 위해
so as to make your stay all the more convenient.

Unit 037-040
Preview

Unit39-b

All reservations will require.
모든 예약들은 필요로 할 것입니다.

All reservations will require

100달러의 보증금을
a $100 security deposit.

All reservations will require a $100 security deposit

주요 신용카드로 결제를 하려면
to be made with a major credit card.

All reservations will require a $100 security deposit to be made with a major credit card

예약이 될 때
at the time of the reservation is made.

Unit39-c

We must remind guests.
저희는 고객들에게 상기 시켜야 합니다.

We must remind guests

고객들은 요구 받을 것이라는 것을
that those will be required.

We must remind guests that those

예약에 지정된 것보다 3일 혹은 그 이상을 일찍 체크아웃 하시는
checking out 3 or more days earlier than specified on their reservation

will be required.

We must remind guests that those checking out 3 or more days earlier than specified on their reservation will be required

추가로 2박 비용을 판매세금까지 더해서 지불하는 것을
to pay for 2 additional nights' accommodation plus sales tax.

Unit 037-040
Preview

We must remind guests that,

> 7월과 8월에는
> **during July and August,** ⊕

those checking out 3 or more days earlier than specified on their reservation will be required to pay for 2 additional nights' accommodation plus sales tax.

We must remind guests that, during July and August, those checking out 3 or more days earlier than specified on their reservation will be required to pay for 2 additional nights' accommodation plus sales tax,

> 여름 성수기 때문에
> **due to the busy nature of the summer.** ⊕

Unit40-a

I am writing to say and am very interested in.

저는 말하려고 하며 또한 매우 관심 있습니다.

I am writing to say

이번 여름 몇 달 동안 당신의 도시에서 머물 것이라는 것을
that I will be in your city for several months this summer

and am very interested in.

I am writing to say that I will be in your city for several months this summer and am very interested in

펜트 하우스 스위트룸을 사용하는 것에
acquiring the use of your penthouse suite.

I am writing to say that I will be in your city for several months this summer and am very interested in acquiring the use of your penthouse suite

제가 머무는 기간 동안
for the duration of my stay.

Unit 037-040
Preview

Unit40-b

My reason is a pro golf competition.
이유는 프로 골프 대회 때문입니다.

My reason

나라 중 그 곳에 가는
for venturing out to your part of the country

is a pro golf competition.

My reason for venturing out to your part of the country is a pro golf competition

7월 8일에 하는
on the 8th of July.

My reason for venturing out to your part of the country is a pro golf competition on the 8th of July

제가 참가할 예정인
that I will be taking part in.

Unit40-c

I would like to remind you.
당신에게 상기시키고 싶습니다.

I would like to remind you

제가 항공편을 통해 들락날락 할 것이라는 것을
that I will be flying in and out

I would like to remind you that, I will be flying in and out

여름 동안 몇 번이고
several times during the summer,

I would like to remind you that,

나의 업무량 때문에
due to my workload,

I will be flying in and out several times during the summer.

I would like to remind you that, due to my workload, I will be flying in and out several times during the summer,

따라서 제 아내와 아이들을 당신의 호텔의 돌봄에 남겨둔다는 것을
thus leaving my wife and children in your care.

Unit 037-040
Preview

Unit40-d

I will place a telephone call and let you know.
제가 전화해서 알려드리겠습니다.

I will place a telephone call

당신에게 ⊕
to you

and let you know.

I will place a telephone call to you

5월 10일까지 ⊕
by the 10th of May

and let you know.

I will place a telephone call to you by the 10th of May

예약의 세부 사항을 확인하기 위해 ⊕
to confirm the details of my reservation

and let you know.

I will place a telephone call to you by the 10th of May to confirm the details of my reservation and let you know

제 신용카드 번호를.
my credit card number.

Unit 37

January 9

Mr. James Park
(이름)

Colombia House Apartments, 231 Benton Boulevard

New York City, NY 02116

Dear Mr. Park,

I have been renting a one-bedroom apartment in your
임대하고 있다
building on Benton Boulevard for the past three years.
(거리명) 지난 3년간
Overall, I have had a pleasant experience living here.
대체로 즐거운 경험
However, on December 27 the heating system in my
그러나 난방 장치
apartment stopped working. I contacted the apartment
고장 났다 연락했다
manager, Ms. Sandra, on that day, and she sent a main-
동격 (이름) 당일
tenance person to fix the problem the following day.
수리공 그 다음날

After spending four hours trying to repair the system, Mr. Wright informed me that he needed to order a part in order to repair it correctly. It took five days for the part to arrive and be installed. While I acknowledge that Ms. Sandra and Mr. Wright did everything they could to fix the problem as quickly as possible, I was still left without heat for almost a week. According to my rental agreement, heat is included in my monthly rent payment; I feel that I should receive financial compensation for my recent hardship. I paid $900 in rent last month, and I feel that I am entitled to $200 in compensation. I was forced to use several space heaters to stay warm over the six days I was without heat. As such, I am expecting my electric bill to be nearly double the usual fee of around $120.

If you have questions, I can be reached at (267) 555-6342.

Sincerely, Mona Sanchez

Unit 37

January 9

Mr. James Park

Colombia House Apartments, 231 Benton Boulevard

New York City, NY 02116

Dear Mr. Park,

I have been renting a one-bedroom apartment in your building on Benton Boulevard for the past three years. Overall, I have had a pleasant experience living here. However, on December 27 the heating system in my apartment stopped working. I contacted the apartment manager, Ms. Sandra, on that day, and she sent a maintenance person to fix the problem the following day.

After spending four hours trying to repair the system, Mr. Wright informed me that he needed to order a part in order to repair it correctly. It took five days for the part to arrive and be installed. While I acknowledge that Ms. Sandra and Mr. Wright did everything they could to fix the problem as quickly as possible, I was still left without heat for almost a week. According to my rental agreement, heat is included in my monthly rent payment; I feel that I should receive financial compensation for my recent hardship. I paid $900 in rent last month, and I feel that I am entitled to $200 in compensation. I was forced to use several space heaters to stay warm over the six days I was without heat. As such, I am expecting my electric bill to be nearly double the usual fee of around $120.

If you have questions, I can be reached at (267) 555-6342.

Sincerely, Mona Sanchez

Unit 38

To: Elena Sanchez <elena@yankees.com>
  (이름)
From: James Park <jpark@columbiahouse.com>
  (이름)
Date: January 10

Subject: Heating problem
  난방 문제

Dear Ms. Sanchez,

I am very sorry to hear that the heating system in your apartment was out of commission for such an extend-
  이용할 수 없는

ed period of time. I understand the inconvenience this must have caused you. I will be mailing you a reimbursement check in the amount that you requested. You have been a loyal tenant, and I hope that will continue well into the future.

Sincerely,

James Park

Owner, Columbia House Apartments

Unit 38

To: Elena Sanchez <elena@yankees.com>

From: James Park <jpark@columbiahouse.com>

Date: January 10

Subject: Heating problem

Dear Ms. Sanchez,

I am very sorry to hear that the heating system in your apartment was out of commission for such an extended period of time. I understand the inconvenience this must have caused you. I will be mailing you a reimbursement check in the amount that you requested. You have been a loyal tenant, and I hope that will continue well into the future.

Sincerely,

James Park

Owner, Columbia House Apartments

Unit 39

The Sunshine Hotel is pleased that you are considering coming to stay with us for a few nights and we have designed this brochure to assist you in the room reservation process so as to make your stay all the more convenient. The Sunshine Hotel offers a wide array of facilities for the pleasure of its guests as well as several degrees of room to choose from, varying from simple double rooms, to suites, to the penthouse. However, all reservations will require a $100 security deposit to be made with a major credit card at the time of the reservation is made.

While making your reservation, you will be asked about the kind of room you would like to stay in as well as the period of time you will be with us. Please specify the exact date you will be arriving and leaving while keeping in mind that you should confirm your reservation one week before your arrival by phone. Unconfirmed rooms may be given to other guests as the need arises. Guests are reminded that they must arrive by 7P.M. on the day of the reservation in order to claim their room.

We must remind guests that during July and August those checking out 3 or more days earlier than specified on their reservation will be required to pay for 2 additional nights' accommodation plus sales tax, due to the busy nature of the summer.

We look forward to your stay.

Unit 39

The Sunshine Hotel is pleased that you are considering coming to stay with us for a few nights and we have designed this brochure to assist you in the room reservation process so as to make your stay all the more convenient. The Sunshine Hotel offers a wide array of facilities for the pleasure of its guests as well as several degrees of room to choose from, varying from simple double rooms, to suites, to the penthouse. However, all reservations will require a $100 security deposit to be made with a major credit card at the time of the reservation is made.

While making your reservation, you will be asked about the kind of room you would like to stay in as well as the period of time you will be with us. Please specify the exact date you will be arriving and leaving while keeping in mind that you should confirm your reservation one week before your arrival by phone. Unconfirmed rooms may be given to other guests as the need arises. Guests are reminded that they must arrive by 7P.M. on the day of the reservation in order to claim their room.

We must remind guests that during July and August those checking out 3 or more days earlier than specified on their reservation will be required to pay for 2 additional nights' accommodation plus sales tax, due to the busy nature of the summer.

We look forward to your stay.

Unit 40

Dear Sunshine Hotel,

My name is Gregg Jarvis, and I am writing to say that I will be in your city for several months this summer and am very interested in acquiring the use of your penthouse suite for the duration of my stay. My family will be accompanying me, and therefore I will need the largest facilities you have to accommodate us. My reason for venturing out to your part of the country is a pro golf competition on the 8th of July that I will be taking part in. However, since my wife really likes the city, we have decided to spend the entire summer there.

Our extended date of arrival is the 30th of May, and we

are planning to stay until the 2nd of September. I would like to remind you that, due to my workload, I will be flying in and out several times during the summer, thus leaving my wife and children in your care. I trust that they will be well looked after.

I will place a telephone call to you by the 10th of May to confirm the details of my reservation and let you know my credit card number. I look forward to hearing precisely what services and specials you will be able to entertain my family with. Thank you for your attention, and I look forward to a prompt reply.

Gregg Jarvis

Unit 40

Dear Sunshine Hotel,

My name is Gregg Jarvis, and I am writing to say that I will be in your city for several months this summer and am very interested in acquiring the use of your penthouse suite for the duration of my stay. My family will be accompanying me, and therefore I will need the largest facilities you have to accommodate us. My reason for venturing out to your part of the country is a pro golf competition on the 8th of July that I will be taking part in. However, since my wife really likes the city, we have decided to spend the entire summer there.

Our extended date of arrival is the 30th of May, and we

are planning to stay until the 2nd of September. I would like to remind you that, due to my workload, I will be flying in and out several times during the summer, thus leaving my wife and children in your care. I trust that they will be well looked after.

I will place a telephone call to you by the 10th of May to confirm the details of my reservation and let you know my credit card number. I look forward to hearing precisely what services and specials you will be able to entertain my family with. Thank you for your attention, and I look forward to a prompt reply.

Gregg Jarvis

Unit 041-044
Preview

Unit41-a

I have been investigating.
저는 알아보고 있습니다.

I have been investigating

다른 선택들을
other options.

I have been investigating other options

참가자들을 위한 호텔 숙소에 대한
for hotel accommodations for participants.

I have been investigating other options for hotel accommodations for participants

다가오는 보안 회담의
in the upcoming security conference.

Baybeach 호텔이 우리의 예약을 취소했기 때문에
Since the Baybeach Hotel canceled our arrangement,

I have been investigating other options for hotel accommodations for participants in the upcoming security conference.

Unit41-b

It is quite late.
꽤 늦었습니다.

It is quite late

최고의 단체 할인가를 찾는 것이
to find the best group rates.

It is quite late to find the best group rates

회담이 두 달도 채 남지 않았기 때문에
since the conference is only less than two months away.

Unit 041-044
Preview

Unit41-c

We would have to cover.
우리는 포함해야 합니다.

We would have to cover

회의장소로 셔틀 버스 서비스를 제공하는 비용을
the expense of providing shuttle service to the conference site.

그러나 그 호텔은 중심 상업 지역 밖에 있기 때문에,
But, as that is outside the central business district,

we would have to cover the expense of providing shuttle service to the conference site.

가장 싼 요금은 Meridian 호텔입니다
The cheapest rate was at the Meridian Hotel,

but, as that is outside the central business district, we would have to cover the expense of providing shuttle service to the conference site.

The cheapest rate

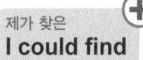
제가 찾은
I could find

was at the Meridian Hotel, but, as that is outside the central business district, we would have to cover the expense of providing shuttle service to the conference site.

Unit42-a

I am inclined.
저는 하고 싶습니다.

I am inclined

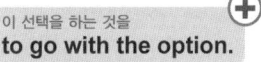
이 선택을 하는 것을
to go with the option.

I am inclined to go with the option

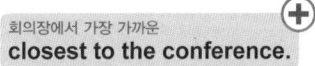
회의장에서 가장 가까운
closest to the conference.

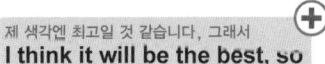
제 생각엔 최고일 것 같습니다, 그래서
I think it will be the best, so

I am inclined to go with the option closest to the conference.

Unit 041–044
Preview

I think it will be the best

편리한 호텔을 예약하는 것이
to book the convenient hotel,

so I am inclined to go with the option closest to the conference.

Unit42-b

They will probably save enough.
그들은 아마도 충분히 아낄 겁니다.

They will probably save enough

그들의 교통비를 지불하기 위해
to pay for their own transportation.

They will probably save enough to pay for their own transportation

회의장으로 가는
to the conference.

만약 그들이 자율적으로 Meridian 호텔을 예약하는 것을 선택한다면,
If they choose to book the Meridian Hotel independently,

they will probably save enough to pay for their own transportation to the conference.

Unit42-c

I think we need to be careful.
제 생각엔 우리는 꼭 신경 쓸 필요가 있습니다.

I think we need to be careful

모두에게 동시에 알리는 것에
to inform everyone at the same time.

I think we need to be careful to inform everyone at the same time,

그리하여 참가자들이 같은 기회를 갖도록
so that the participants have the same chance.

I think we need to be careful to inform everyone at the same time, so that the participants have the same chance

단체 할인가로 방을 얻을 수 있는
to obtain rooms at the group rate.

Unit 041-044
Preview

Unit43-a

We are currently looking for someone.
우리는 누군가를 현재 찾고 있습니다.

We are currently looking for someone

마지막 편집을 수행할
to perform final edits.

We are currently looking for someone to perform final edits

Great Life의 간소화한 판에서의
on a simplified version of the Great Life.

We are currently looking for someone to perform final edits on a simplified version of the Great Life

Nicolas Maggie에 의해 쓰인
by Nicolas Maggie.

Unit43-b

The work will involve.
작업은 포함할 겁니다.

The work will involve

확실하게 해두었는지 확인하는 것을
checking to make sure.

The work will involve checking to make sure

어휘들이 너무 어렵지 않은지
the vocabulary is not too difficult.

The work will involve checking to make sure the vocabulary

간소화된 판에 있는
in the simplified version.

is not too difficult.

The work will involve checking to make sure the vocabulary in the simplified version is not too difficult

목표 독자들에게
for the target audience.

Unit 041-044
Preview

The work will involve checking to make sure the vocabulary in the simplified version is not too difficult for the target audience,

그리고 문법과 발음이 올바른지
and that grammar and pronunciation are correct.

Unit44-a

We will continue to try.
우리는 계속 노력할 것입니다.

We will continue to try

방법을 찾기 위해
to find a way.

We will continue to try to find a way

품질 높은 서비스를 유지하기 위한
to maintain the high quality service.

We will continue to try to find a way to maintain the high quality service

우리가 제공하는
we provide.

We will continue to try to find a way to maintain the high quality service we provide,

가격 올리기나 고객 제공 사이즈를 줄이는 것 없이
without increasing prices or reducing customer serving size.

Unit44-b

I suggest.
저는 제안합니다.

I suggest

우리가 다른 방법을 찾는 것을
that we find other ways.

I suggest that we find other ways

그 안에서 서비스의 수준을 올리기 위한
in which to maintain the level of service.

Unit 041-044
Preview

I suggest that we find other ways in which to maintain the level of service

우리가 제공하는 ⊕
we provide.

I suggest that

비용을 전가하는 것을 피하기 위해서 ⊕
in order to avoid passing these costs,

we find other ways in which to maintain the level of service we provide.

I suggest that in order to avoid passing these costs

우리의 소중한 고객들에게 ⊕
on to our valued customers,

we find other ways in which to maintain the level of service we provide.

Unit44-c

We will expand.
우리는 확장할 것입니다.

We will expand

우리의 사업을 ➕
our business.

We will expand our business

덜 부담스런 음식서비스를 제공함으로써 ➕
by providing less upscale catering services.

We will expand our business by providing less upscale catering services

소규모 기업들에게 ➕
to smaller companies.

We will expand our business by providing less upscale catering services to smaller companies

우리의 비싼 서비스를 감당할 수 없는 ➕
that can't afford our more lavish services.

Unit 41

To: Larry Brown <larryb@siliconsec.com>

From: Clara Muller <clara@siliconsec.com>

Date: November 11

Subject: Hotel selection

Dear Larry,

Since the Baybeach Hotel canceled our arrangement, I have been investigating other options for hotel accommodations for participants in the upcoming security conference. Unfortunately, it is quite late to find the best group rates since the conference is only less than two months away. The Grove Inn is right across the street from the conference center location and can offer us a reasonable group rate ($120 per night). However, they can only guarantee us 30 rooms at this price; any participants over that number will have to pay the normal seasonal rate of $180. The Skyview Lodge is only a little further away and can provide us with 50 rooms, but the price is much higher than either Baybeach or Grove. The cheapest rate I could find was at the Meridian Hotel, but, as that is outside the central business district, we would have to cover the expense of providing shuttle service to the conference site.

Please let me know what you suggest, and I will make final arrangements as quickly as possible.

Clara Muller

Unit 41

To: Larry Brown <larryb@siliconsec.com>

From: Clara Muller <clara@siliconsec.com>

Date: November 11

Subject: Hotel selection

Dear Larry,

Since the Baybeach Hotel canceled our arrangement, I have been investigating other options for hotel accommodations for participants in the upcoming security conference. Unfortunately, it is quite late to find the best group rates since the conference is only less than two months away. The Grove Inn is right across the street from the conference center location and can offer us a reasonable group rate ($120 per night). However, they can only guarantee us 30 rooms at this price; any participants over that number will have to pay the normal seasonal rate of $180. The Skyview Lodge is only a little further away and can provide us with 50 rooms, but the price is much higher than either Baybeach or Grove. The cheapest rate I could find was at the Meridian Hotel, but, as that is outside the central business district, we would have to cover the expense of providing shuttle service to the conference site.

Please let me know what you suggest, and I will make final arrangements as quickly as possible.

Clara Muller

Unit 42

To: Clara Muller <clara@siliconsec.com>

From: Larry Brown <larryb@siliconsec.com>

Date: November 11

Subject: RE: Hotel selection

Hi Clara,

Thank you for going to so much extra trouble. Baybeach Hotel's renovation project certainly comes at an inconvenient time for us. I think it will be the best to book the convenient hotel, so I am inclined to go with the option closest to the conference. We currently have about 45 registrations, so the majority of attendees will pay the same rate as they would have at the Baybeach. The others will have the option of staying further away; if they choose to book the Meridian Hotel independently, they will probably save enough to pay for their own transportation to the conference.

Please do not release this information until after the arrangements have been confirmed. I think we need to be careful to inform everyone at the same time, so that the participants have the same chance to obtain rooms at the group rate.

Thanks again, and I am looking forward to seeing you at the conference.

Larry Brown

Unit 42

To: Clara Muller <clara@siliconsec.com>

From: Larry Brown <larryb@siliconsec.com>

Date: November 11

Subject: RE: Hotel selection

Hi Clara,

Thank you for going to so much extra trouble. Baybeach Hotel's renovation project certainly comes at an inconvenient time for us. I think it will be the best to book the convenient hotel, so I am inclined to go with the option closest to the conference. We currently have about 45 registrations, so the majority of attendees will pay the same rate as they would have at the Baybeach. The others will have the option of staying further away; if they choose to book the Meridian Hotel independently, they will probably save enough to pay for their own transportation to the conference.

Please do not release this information until after the arrangements have been confirmed. I think we need to be careful to inform everyone at the same time, so that the participants have the same chance to obtain rooms at the group rate.

Thanks again, and I am looking forward to seeing you at the conference.

Larry Brown

Unit 43

Dear Mr. Timmons,

Donald Cho has recommended that I contact you regarding editing work.

We are currently looking for someone to perform final edits on a simplified version of the Great Life by Nicolas Maggie. It consists of 135 pages including glossary, illustrations. The simplified version is aimed at typical 3rd-5th grade elementary school students; it has also already been partially edited. The work will involve checking to make sure the vocabulary in the simplified version is not too difficult for the target audience, and that grammar and pronunciation are correct. Usually Donald returns the hard copy with amendments highlighted - this helps us make a final decision about each change. We could aim to mail the work out to you during the first week of August.

Please would you be able to tell me:

- If you are interested in doing the work
- How long you think it will take
- How much you would charge to do it

Please, could you get back to me as soon as possible and let me know if it is possible for you to do the work?

Many thanks & kind regards

Irene

Noble Publishing Inc.

Unit 43

Dear Mr. Timmons,

Donald Cho has recommended that I contact you regarding editing work.

We are currently looking for someone to perform final edits on a simplified version of the Great Life by Nicolas Maggie. It consists of 135 pages including glossary, illustrations. The simplified version is aimed at typical 3rd-5th grade elementary school students; it has also already been partially edited.

The work will involve checking to make sure the vocabulary in the simplified version is not too difficult for the target audience, and that grammar and pronunciation are correct. Usually Donald returns the hard copy with amendments highlighted - this helps us make a final decision about each change. We could aim to mail the work out to you during the first week of August.

Please would you be able to tell me:

- If you are interested in doing the work
- How long you think it will take
- How much you would charge to do it

Please, could you get back to me as soon as possible and let me know if it is possible for you to do the work?

Many thanks & kind regards

Irene

Noble Publishing Inc.

Unit 44

To: Comfort Caterers employees

From: Head Office

Date: August 20

Re: Difficult decisions

Comfort Caterers, Inc. has been vital to the business community for more than 50 years, catering dinners and lunches for executive parties in and around the New York area. Our clientele base is made up of large successful companies who are accustomed to only the best and highest quality meals. As you are aware, global food prices are skyrocketing. The price of rice alone has more than doubled in the past year, and all dairy products including cheeses have dramatically increased in price. However, we will continue to try to find a way to maintain the high quality service we provide, without increasing prices or reducing customer serving size. I suggest that in order to avoid passing these costs on to our valued customers, we find other ways in which to maintain the level of service we provide. Sacrifices will have to be made. The company will open earlier and close later. Also, we will expand our business by providing less upscale catering services to smaller companies that can't afford our more lavish services. This, for the time being, will help us finance the higher costs of food.

Unit 44

To: Comfort Caterers employees

From: Head Office

Date: August 20

Re: Difficult decisions

Comfort Caterers, Inc. has been vital to the business community for more than 50 years, catering dinners and lunches for executive parties in and around the New York area. Our clientele base is made up of large successful companies who are accustomed to only the best and highest quality meals.

As you are aware, global food prices are skyrocketing. The price of rice alone has more than doubled in the past year, and all dairy products including cheeses have dramatically increased in price. However, we will continue to try to find a way to maintain the high quality service we provide, without increasing prices or reducing customer serving size. I suggest that in order to avoid passing these costs on to our valued customers, we find other ways in which to maintain the level of service we provide. Sacrifices will have to be made. The company will open earlier and close later. Also, we will expand our business by providing less upscale catering services to smaller companies that can't afford our more lavish services. This, for the time being, will help us finance the higher costs of food.

Unit 045-048
Preview

Unit45-a

I would like to express.
저는 표현하고 싶습니다.

I would like to express

깊은 감사를
my deepest appreciation.

I would like to express my deepest appreciation

훌륭한 고객 서비스에
for the excellent customer service.

I would like to express my deepest appreciation for the excellent customer service

제가 최근에 받은
I recently received.

I would like to express my deepest appreciation for the excellent customer service I recently received

당신의 직원들 중 한 명으로부터
from one of your employees.

Unit45-b

She checked.
그녀는 확인했습니다.

She checked

그 물품을 ⊕
for the item.

She checked for the item

매장과 창고 둘 다에서 ⊕
both on the sales floor and in the warehouse area.

She checked for the item both on the sales floor and in the warehouse area

보기 위해 ⊕
to see.

She checked for the item both on the sales floor and in the warehouse area to see

더 있는지를 ⊕
if there were any more.

Unit 045-048
Preview

Unit45-c

She kindly filled out a form.
그녀는 친절하게 서식을 작성했습니다.

She kindly filled out a form

물건을 요청하는
requesting the item.

She kindly filled out a form requesting the item

내가 받게 될
be held for me.

She kindly filled out a form requesting the item be held for me

매장이 추가된 물건들을 받으면
if the store receives another shipment.

그녀가 어떤 것도 찾지 못하자,
When she was unable to find any,

she kindly filled out a form requesting the item be held for me if the store receives another shipment.

Unit45-d

Ms. Becky later tracked me down.
Ms. Becky는 저를 뒤쫓아 왔습니다.

Ms. Becky later tracked me down

다른 매장으로
in another department.

Ms. Becky later tracked me down in another department

저에게 알려주기 위해
to let me know.

Ms. Becky later tracked me down in another department to let me know

그녀가 커피 테이블을 발견했다고
that she had found the coffee table.

Unit 045-048
Preview

Ms. Becky later tracked me down in another department to let me know that she had found the coffee table

제가 원했던
I wanted.

Ms. Becky later tracked me down in another department to let me know that she had found the coffee table I wanted

배달 상품 도착 구역에서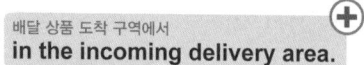
in the incoming delivery area.

Unit46-a

The red tape is burdensome and is becoming worse.
불필요한 요식 행위는 부담스럽고 점점 악화되고 있습니다.

The red tape

이곳에서 비즈니스를 수행하는데 관련된
involved in conducting business here

is burdensome and is becoming worse.

The red tape involved in conducting business here is **unacceptably** (받아들일 수 없게) burdensome and is **apparently** (외견적으로) becoming worse.

Unit46-b

I'm requesting approval.
저는 승인을 요청합니다.

I'm requesting approval **for funds to contract.** (계약 자금을 위한)

I'm requesting approval for funds to contract **with a private transportation company.** (민영 운송 업체와의)

Unit 045-048
Preview

I'm requesting approval for funds to contract with a private transportation company

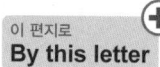
이 위기를 극복하기 위한 시도로써
in an attempt to get over this crisis.

이 편지로
By this letter

I'm requesting approval for funds to contract with a private transportation company in an attempt to get over this crisis.

Unit47-a

Mr. Barish spent only one hour, and left.

Mr. Barish는 한 시간만을 사용하고 떠났습니다.

Mr. Barish spent only one hour

사진을 찍는 데에
taking pictures,

and left.

Mr. Barish spent only one hour taking pictures, and left

이벤트가 끝나기 한참 전에
well before the event had ended.

사전에 합의한 시간과 다르게,
Contrary to the prior agreed time,

Mr. Barish spent only one hour taking pictures, and left well before the event had ended.

Unit47-b

I believe.
저는 생각합니다.

I believe

부당하다고
it is unfair.

I believe it is unfair

청구되는 것이
to be charged.

Unit 045-048
Preview

I believe it is unfair to be charged

세 시간의 서비스에 대해
for three hours of service.

I believe it is unfair to be charged for three hours of service

오직 한 시간만이 제공되었을 때
when only one hour was provided.

Unit47-c I am prepared.
저는 준비하고 있습니다.

I am prepared

100달러를 지불하려고
to pay this $100.

I am prepared to pay this $100

훌륭한 서비스 때문에
because of the excellent service.

I am prepared to pay this $100 because of the excellent service

여러 차례 당신 회사가 제공한
your company has provided me several times.

I am prepared to pay this $100 because of the excellent service your company has provided me several times

지금까지
in the past.

Unit48-a

Best Ontario Swim Club is not liable.
Best Ontario Swim Club은 책임이 없습니다.

Best Ontario Swim Club is not liable

분실 혹은 손상에 대한
for loss of or damage.

Best Ontario Swim Club is not liable for loss of or damage

모든 개인 소지품의
to any personal possessions.

Unit 045-048
Preview

Best Ontario Swim Club is not liable for loss of or damage to any personal possessions

이곳의 시설들에서
at its facilities.

인증된 회원 규정과 동봉된 회원 계약서 양쪽에 설명된 것과 같이,
As stated on both the sign listing club regulations and the enclosed member's contract,

Best Ontario Swim Club is not liable for loss of or damage to any personal possessions at its facilities.

As stated on both the sign listing club regulations

라커룸에 있는
in the locker room

and the enclosed member's contract,

가입할 때 계약한
which you signed when joining the club,

Best Ontario Swim Club is not liable for loss of or damage to any personal possessions at its facilities.

Unit48-b

It would be most unfortunate.
몹시 유감스럽습니다.

It would be most unfortunate

이 사건이 우리의 관계를 망쳐 버릴 까봐
if this incident were to spoil our relationship.

지금껏 당신이 신의 있는 회원 이었기 때문에,
As you have been a faithful member,

it would be most unfortunate if this incident were to spoil our relationship.

Unit 045-048
Preview

As you have been a faithful member

여러 해 동안 Best Ontario Swim Club에서
at Best Ontario Swim Club for several years,

it would be most unfortunate if this incident were to spoil our relationship.

Unit48-c

Let us offer you.
당신에게 제안토록 해주세요.

Let us offer you

무료의 개인 사물함 자물쇠 혹은 무료로 추가의 한달 멤버십을
a complimentary lock for your locker or an extra month of membership free of charge.

문제점들과 경비지출을 만회하기 위해
To make up for some of the trouble and expense,

let us offer you a complimentary lock for your locker or an extra month of membership free of charge.

To make up for some of the trouble and expense

당신이 처하게 된
you incurred

, let us offer you a complimentary lock for your locker or an extra month of membership free of charge.

To make up for some of the trouble and expense you incurred

새 노트북을 구입하면서
in getting new laptop computer,

let us offer you a complimentary lock for your locker or an extra month of membership free of charge.

Unit 45

Dear General Manager,

I would like to express my deepest appreciation for the excellent customer service I recently received from one of your employees. Ms. Becky was working at your Mega Store when I came in on February 20. I was hoping to purchase a coffee table that was on sale, but it appeared to be sold out. I approached Ms. Becky at the Customer Service Department and asked for help. She checked for the item both ❶ on the sales floor and ❷ in the warehouse area to see if there were any more. When she was unable to find any, she kindly filled out a form ==requesting the item be held for me== if the store receives another shipment. I then continued to shop elsewhere in the store.

Ms. Becky later tracked me down in another department to let me know that she had found the coffee table ==I wanted== in the incoming delivery area. She even offered to bring it up to the register so that I could continue to shop. I was very impresses by Ms. Becky's willingness to help and am grateful for her initiative in finding the table for me.

I hope that you will recognize and commend Ms. Becky for her excellent work. She was extremely kind and helpful to me, and I am sure that she helps out countless customers on a daily basis.

Best regards,

Samantha Arroyo

Unit 45

Dear General Manager,

I would like to express my deepest appreciation for the excellent customer service I recently received from one of your employees. Ms. Becky was working at your Mega Store when I came in on February 20. I was hoping to purchase a coffee table that was on sale, but it appeared to be sold out. I approached Ms. Becky at the Customer Service Department and asked for help. She checked for the item both on the sales floor and in the warehouse area to see if there were any more. When she was unable to find any, she kindly filled out a form requesting the item be held for me if the store receives another shipment. I then continued to shop elsewhere in the store.

Ms. Becky later tracked me down in another department to let me know that she had found the coffee table I wanted in the incoming delivery area. She even offered to bring it up to the register so that I could continue to shop. I was very impresses by Ms. Becky's willingness to help and am grateful for her initiative in finding the table for me.

I hope that you will recognize and commend Ms. Becky for her excellent work. She was extremely kind and helpful to me, and I am sure that she helps out countless customers on a daily basis.

Best regards,

Samantha Arroyo

Unit 46

To: Frederick Bergen, CEO
(이름)

From: Danny Henson, Managing Director
(이름)   상무 이사

Date: October 20

Dear Frederick Bergen,

I'm sorry to say that I have been quite frustrated with
                                              낙담한
the progress here. When we opened as promised six
이곳의 진전에 대해   약속한 바와 같이
months ago, we enjoyed low wage scale and productive
                          낮은 임금 규모   생산적인
workers. The red tape involved in conducting business
          불필요한 요식 행위 이곳에서 비즈니스를 수행하는데 관련된
here, however, is unacceptably burdensome and is ap-
      하지만   받아들일 수 없이   부담 스러운

parently becoming worse.

More specifically, recently it has been very challenging to arrange export shipping. All forms of transportation, including trains, trucks, and ships fail to keep to their schedules, and many do not even depart, although they are scheduled to. We need to maintain good client relationships by keeping our promises with them and keeping productivity up. By this letter I'm requesting approval for funds to contract with a private transportation company in an attempt to get over this crisis. Let me try this way for another couple months. If things don't improve, we should consider withdrawing from all manufacturing activity here.

I hope you understand the urgency of this situation and can give me a prompt reply. I have a company in mind. They are ready to move as soon as we contract with them.

Unit 46

To: Frederick Bergen, CEO

From: Danny Henson, Managing Director

Date: October 20

Dear Frederick Bergen,

I'm sorry to say that I have been quite frustrated with the progress here. When we opened as promised six months ago, we enjoyed low wage scale and productive workers. The red tape involved in conducting business here, however, is unacceptably burdensome and is apparently becoming worse.

More specifically, recently it has been very challenging to arrange export shipping. All forms of transportation, including trains, trucks, and ships fail to keep to their schedules, and many do not even depart, although they are scheduled to. We need to maintain good client relationships by keeping our promises with them and keeping productivity up. By this letter I'm requesting approval for funds to contract with a private transportation company in an attempt to get over this crisis. Let me try this way for another couple months. If things don't improve, we should consider withdrawing from all manufacturing activity here.

I hope you understand the urgency of this situation and can give me a prompt reply. I have a company in mind. They are ready to move as soon as we contract with them.

Unit 47

Angela Brown's Photography Service

325 South Oak, Pasadena, CA 90020

December 27

Dear Ms. Brown,

I would like to dispute the total amount I was charged for photography services rendered on December 13; on that day, your assistant, Greg Barish, visited the Ashland area branch of my company to take pictures of a corporate event. Contrary to the prior agreed time, Mr. Barish spent only one hour taking pictures, and left well before the event had ended. When I asked Mr. Barish where he was going, he stated that he had another assignment that day.

The bill I received in the mail on December 17 was for $100: three hours of service at $25 per hour and $25 for miscellaneous costs including travel and set-up. I believe it is unfair to be charged for three hours of service when only one hour was provided. However, I am prepared to pay this $100 because of the excellent service your company has provided me several times in the past. This time, I was lucky enough to have a colleague of mine take pictures of the event after Mr. Barish's departure. Attached to this letter is a check for $50. If you would like to discuss this matter further, please contact me at 555-8655.

Regards,

Robert Sundstrom

Unit 47

Angela Brown's Photography Service

325 South Oak, Pasadena, CA 90020

December 27

Dear Ms. Brown,

I would like to dispute the total amount I was charged for photography services rendered on December 13; on that day, your assistant, Greg Barish, visited the Ashland area branch of my company to take pictures of a corporate event. Contrary to the prior agreed time, Mr. Barish spent only one hour taking pictures, and left well before the event had ended. When I asked Mr. Barish where he was going, he stated that he had another assignment that day.

The bill I received in the mail on December 17 was for $100: three hours of service at $25 per hour and $25 for miscellaneous costs including travel and set-up. I believe it is unfair to be charged for three hours of service when only one hour was provided. However, I am prepared to pay this $100 because of the excellent service your company has provided me several times in the past. This time, I was lucky enough to have a colleague of mine take pictures of the event after Mr. Barish's departure. Attached to this letter is a check for $50. If you would like to discuss this matter further, please contact me at 555-8655.

Regards,

Robert Sundstrom

Unit 48

Mr. Chris Duncan
　(이름)

317 New Brunswick St. #234

Toronto, Ontario M1B 2DA
　(도시명)　온타리오(주명)

Dear Mr. Duncan:

Thank you for writing to us about your visit to the Best
　　　　　　　　　　　당신의 방문에 관해

Ontario Swim Club on July 14. I'm sorry to read about the
(수영장명)　　　　　　　　　유감이다

loss of your laptop computer during your visit. I fully un-
노트북의 분실에 관해 읽게 되어서　　방문하는 동안　　충분히

derstand that your loss is both inconvenient and costly.
　　　　　　　　　불편할 뿐만 아니라 비용도 든다

While we highly value our clients at Best Ontario Swim
우리는 고객들이 소중하지만

Club, I regret that we cannot reimburse you for the cost
유감스럽게 생각하다　　　　　　배상하다　　　　비용

of new laptop computer. As stated on both the sign listing club regulations in the locker room and the enclosed member's contract, which you signed when joining the club, Best Ontario Swim Club is not liable for loss of or damage to any personal possessions at its facilities. As you have been a faithful member at Best Ontario Swim Club for several years, it would be most unfortunate if this incident were to spoil our relationship. To make up for some of the trouble and expense you incurred in getting new laptop computer, let us offer you a complimentary lock for your locker or an extra month of membership free of charge. Just bring in this letter on your next visit, and we'll provide you with a lock or a membership voucher.

Sincerely,

Kevin Pedroia, Manager

Customer Relations

Unit 48

Mr. Chris Duncan

317 New Brunswick St. #234

Toronto, Ontario M1B 2DA

Dear Mr. Duncan:

Thank you for writing to us about your visit to the Best Ontario Swim Club on July 14. I'm sorry to read about the loss of your laptop computer during your visit. I fully understand that your loss is both inconvenient and costly. While we highly value our clients at Best Ontario Swim Club, I regret that we cannot reimburse you for the cost of new laptop computer. As stated on both the sign listing club regulations in the locker room and the enclosed member's contract, which you signed when joining the club, Best Ontario Swim Club is not liable for loss of or damage to any personal possessions at its facilities.

As you have been a faithful member at Best Ontario Swim Club for several years, it would be most unfortunate if this incident were to spoil our relationship. To make up for some of the trouble and expense you incurred in getting new laptop computer, let us offer you a complimentary lock for your locker or an extra month of membership free of charge. Just bring in this letter on your next visit, and we'll provide you with a lock or a membership voucher.

Sincerely,

Kevin Pedroia, Manager

Customer Relations

Unit 049-052
Preview

Unit49-a

I was out of the country and was only recently able to try.

저는 해외에 있었고 최근에야 시도해 보았습니다.

I was out of the country

거의 두 달간을 출장으로
on business for nearly two months

and was only recently able to try.

I was out of the country on business for nearly two months and was only recently able to try

제품을 사용하는 것을
using the product.

제가 3월 31일에 사다리를 구입하긴 했지만,
Although I purchased the ladder on March 31,

I was out of the country on business for nearly two months and was only recently able to try using the product.

Unit50-a

Our return policy states.
저희 반품 방침은 명시합니다.

Our return policy states

어떤 이유가 있어도 교환이 될 것이라는 것을
that it may be returned to the store for any reason.

Our return policy states that

만약 제품이 한달 내에 구매가 되었다면
if the product was purchased less than one month ago,

it may be returned to the store for any reason.

Our return policy states that if the product was purchased less than one month ago, it may be returned to the store for any reason

판매 영수증이 제시되고 제품이 포장되어 있다면
if a sales receipt is presented and the product is packing.

Unit 049-052
Preview

Our return policy states that if the product was purchased less than one month ago, it may be returned to the store for any reason if a sales receipt is presented and the product is packing

제품의 본래 포장 재료로
in its original packing materials.

Unit50-b Purchases may be returned.
구매는 반품될 수 있습니다.

Purchases

한 달이 지나서 이루어진
made more than one month ago

may be returned.

Purchases made more than one month ago may be returned

만약 물품이 손상되었거나 결함이 있었다면
if the product was damaged or defective.

Purchases made more than one month ago may be returned if the product was damaged or defective

구매 시점에서
at the time of purchase.

Unit50-c

This code must be presented.
이 번호는 제시되어야만 합니다.

This code must be presented

점포 영수증과 함께
along with a store receipt.

This code must be presented along with a store receipt

물품이 점포로 반환될 때
when the product is returned to the store.

Unit 049-052
Preview

Unit50-d

Please fill out the attached questionnaire.
첨부된 설문지를 작성해 주십시오.

Please fill out the attached questionnaire

당신의 경험에 대한
about your experience.

Please fill out the attached questionnaire about your experience

저희 고객 서비스와의
with our customer service department.

저희가 당신을 미래에 더 잘 도와드릴 수 있도록,
To help us serve you better in the future,

please fill out the attached questionnaire about your experience with our customer service department.

Unit51-a

It's not every day.
흔한 일이 아닙니다.

It's not every day

제가 서비스에 매우 감명 받는 것은
that I'm so impressed with the service.

It's not every day that I'm so impressed with the service

제가 받은
I receive.

저는 이런 종류의 편지를 쓰는 것에 익숙하지 않습니다만
I'm not used to writing this sort of letter, but

it's not every day that I'm so impressed with the service I receive.

Unit 049-052
Preview

Unit51-b I was even more impressed.
저는 더 감명 받았습니다.

I was even more impressed

그들이 정확히 나타났을 때
when they showed up exactly.

I was even more impressed
when they showed up exactly

그들이 오리라 말했던 시간에
when they had said they would.

I was even more impressed
when they showed up exactly
when they had said they would

그리고 매우 효과적으로 일을 했을 때
and worked very efficiently.

I was even more impressed when they showed up exactly when they had said they would and worked very efficiently

저희가 가게에 너무 늦게 머물지 않도록
so that we wouldn't have to stay too late in the store.

Unit51-c

I'm enclosing.
저는 동봉합니다.

I'm enclosing

두 개의 식사 상품권을
two gift certificates for a meal.

I'm enclosing two gift certificates for a meal

인근에 있는 제가 제일 좋아하는 프랑스 레스토랑 중에 하나인 Montmartre에서의
at Montmartre, one of my favorite French restaurants in the neighborhood.

Unit 049-052
Preview

제 감사의 표시로,
As a small token of my appreciation,

I'm enclosing two gift certificates for a meal at Montmartre, one of my favorite French restaurants in the neighborhood.

As a small token of my appreciation

당신의 직원들이 저희에게 해준 훌륭한 작업에 대한
for the excellent job your men did for us,

I'm enclosing two gift certificates for a meal at Montmartre, one of my favorite French restaurants in the neighborhood.

Unit52-a

I closely work.
저는 가깝게 일합니다.

I closely work

기자들과
with journalists.

I closely work with journalists

출판, 방송 그리고 온라인 미디어 매체의
from publishers, broadcasts and online media outlets.

I closely work with journalists from publishers, broadcasts and online media outlets,

헤드라인을 제공하면서
providing news leads.

Unit 049-052
Preview

홍보이사인 제 현재 직업으로서
In my current job as public relations director,

I closely work with journalists from publishers, broadcasts and online media outlets, providing news leads.

In my current job as public relations director

보스턴에 있는 Glenn Business 학교에서의
of Glenn Business School in Boston,

I closely work with journalists from publishers, broadcasts and online media outlets, providing news leads.

Unit52-b

I spent several years.
저는 몇 년을 보냈습니다.

I spent several years
베를린에서
in Berlin.

I spent several years in Berlin
마케팅 학생으로서 그리고 나서 인턴으로서
as a marketing student and then as an intern.

I spent several years in Berlin as a marketing student
Munich 대학에서
at Munich University

and then as an intern
베를린 Media Relation Group에서의
at Berlin Media Relation Group.

Unit 049-052
Preview

제 이력서에서 나타나듯이,
As my resume indicates,

I spent several years in Berlin as a marketing student at Munich University and then as an intern at Berlin Media Relation Group.

Unit52-c — My fluency served me well.
제 능숙함은 저에게 많은 도움을 줍니다.

My fluency

특히 만다린 중국어와 영어, 프랑스어에서의
in English, French and Mandarin Chinese in particular

served me well.

My fluency in English, French and Mandarin Chinese in particular served me well

소통하는 데 있어서
in communicating.

My fluency in English, French and Mandarin Chinese in particular served me well in communicating

국제 미디어와
with international media. ⊕

Unit 49

To: customerservice@toolscorp.com

From: Manuel Lamb <manuel@bayercrafts.com>
           (이름)

Date: May 19

Subject: customer service request
              고개 서비스 요청

Dear Sir or Madam:
      관계자, 담당자

I am writing to report a problem with my new 2.5 me-
           문제를 보고하기 위해

ter ladder. The ladder does not sit squarely on the floor
    사다리   반듯하게 맞다

because one of the legs is two centimeters too long.
~때문에   다리 중 하나   2센티미터가 더 길다

Climbing onto a wobbly ladder is very dangerous, so it
올라가다   흔들리는

is unusable. I would appreciate it if you could send a replacement or a refund.
I am sorry it has taken me so long to contact you about this. Although I purchased the ladder on March 31, I was out of the country on business for nearly two months and was only recently able to try using the product. I still have the store receipt which I can supply if required.

Sincerely,

Manuel Lamb

Bayer Craftworks

Unit 49

To: customerservice@toolscorp.com

From: Manuel Lamb <manuel@bayercrafts.com>

Date: May 19

Subject: customer service request

Dear Sir or Madam:

I am writing to report a problem with my new 2.5 meter ladder. The ladder does not sit squarely on the floor because one of the legs is two centimeters too long. Climbing onto a wobbly ladder is very dangerous, so it is unusable. I would appreciate it if you could send a replacement or a refund.

I am sorry it has taken me so long to contact you about this. Although I purchased the ladder on March 31, I was out of the country on business for nearly two months and was only recently able to try using the product. I still have the store receipt which I can supply if required.

Sincerely,

Manuel Lamb

Bayer Craftworks

Unit 50

To: Manuel Lamb <manuel@bayercrafts.com>

From: Christopher Lee <chrislee@toolscorp.com>

Date: May 21 / Subject: RE: customer service request

Dear Mr. Lamb:

Thank you for your feedback on your product. We are sorry that you are experiencing difficulty with your purchase, and we will be happy to provide you with a replacement at no cost.

Our return policy states that if the product was purchased less than one month ago, it may be returned to the store for any reason if a sales receipt is presented and the product is packing in its original packing materials. Purchases made more than one month ago may be returned if the product was damaged or defective at the time of purchase. In this case, a Merchandise Return Form must be filled out. After the form has been filled out and submitted, a Merchandise Return Code will be e-mailed to the customer. This code must be presented along with a store receipt when the product is returned to the store. Original packing materials are not required for damaged or defective products. Please visit our Web site to see the full policy.

I hope this reply has been helpful. To help us serve you better in the future, please fill out the attached questionnaire about your experience with our customer service department. We will send you a store coupon for 10% off your next purchase when we receive your completed questionnaire.

Christopher Lee, Customer Service

Unit 50

To: Manuel Lamb <manuel@bayercrafts.com>

From: Christopher Lee <chrislee@toolscorp.com>

Date: May 21 / Subject: RE: customer service request

Dear Mr. Lamb:

Thank you for your feedback on your product. We are sorry that you are experiencing difficulty with your purchase, and we will be happy to provide you with a replacement at no cost.

Our return policy states that if the product was purchased less than one month ago, it may be returned to the store for any reason if a sales receipt is presented and the product is packing in its original packing materials. Purchases made more than one month ago may be returned if the product was damaged or defective at the time of purchase. In this case, a Merchandise Return Form must be filled out. After the form has been filled out and submitted, a Merchandise Return Code will be e-mailed to the customer. This code must be presented along with a store receipt when the product is returned to the store. Original packing materials are not required for damaged or defective products. Please visit our Web site to see the full policy.

I hope this reply has been helpful. To help us serve you better in the future, please fill out the attached questionnaire about your experience with our customer service department. We will send you a store coupon for 10% off your next purchase when we receive your completed questionnaire.

Christopher Lee, Customer Service

Unit 51

Mike Torre
(이름)

SOS Security
(회사명)

325, Windsor Street, Madison, Wisconsin
매디슨(도시명)위스콘신(주명)

Dear Mr. Torre

My name is Brady little, and I recently had a security system updated in our store. I'm not used to writing this sort of letter, but it's not every day that I'm so impressed with the service I receive.

Two weeks ago two technicians came out to do the work to update our security system. At that time, we were very busy and shorthanded, as one of our salesclerks had called in sick that morning. Your technicians instantly saw the situation we were in and offered to come back after business hours to do the work. I was even more impressed when they showed up exactly when they had said they would and worked very efficiently so that we wouldn't have to stay too late in the store. They were kind enough to explain very patiently how to operate the system. I'm old and far from being mechanically inclined, but they never once expressed any sort of impatience. Needless to say, I was very satisfied with their work.

As a small token of my appreciation for the excellent job your men did for us, I'm enclosing two gift certificates for a meal at Montmartre, one of my favorite French restaurants in the neighborhood. I would very much appreciate it if you would pass my sincere thanks along with these gift certificates.

Best regards,

Brady Little

Unit 51

Mike Torre

SOS Security

325, Windsor Street, Madison, Wisconsin

Dear Mr. Torre

My name is Brady little, and I recently had a security system updated in our store. I'm not used to writing this sort of letter, but it's not every day that I'm so impressed with the service I receive.

Two weeks ago two technicians came out to do the work to update our security system. At that time, we were very busy and shorthanded, as one of our salesclerks had called in sick that morning. Your technicians instantly saw the situation we were in and offered to come back after business hours to do the work. I was even more impressed when they showed up exactly when they had said they would and worked very efficiently so that we wouldn't have to stay too late in the store. They were kind enough to explain very patiently how to operate the system. I'm old and far from being mechanically inclined, but they never once expressed any sort of impatience. Needless to say, I was very satisfied with their work.

As a small token of my appreciation for the excellent job your men did for us, I'm enclosing two gift certificates for a meal at Montmartre, one of my favorite French restaurants in the neighborhood. I would very much appreciate it if you would pass my sincere thanks along with these gift certificates.

Best regards,

Brady Little

Unit 52

To: Jeffrey Connors <jconnors@info.de>
    (이름)
From: Ann Heller ann@glennbiz.com
      (이름)
Subject: My information / Date: January 12
         나의 정보

It was a great pleasure meeting you at the media con-
                                          미디어 총회
ference in Stockholm, Sweden on January 8. Thank you
         (도시명)   (국가명)
for informing me of your company's job vacancy for an
   알려줌   공석
international media liaison. I believe I am an ideal can-
국제 미디어 교섭   이상적인 지원자
didate. In my current job as public relations director of
            현재의   홍보이사
Glenn Business School in Boston, I closely work with
    (학교명)   (도시명)   가깝게
journalists from publishers, broadcasts and online me-
기자   출판   방송   온라인 미디어 매체
dia outlets, providing news leads. In addition, I serve as
        헤드라인을 제공하면서   또한

a technology director of student radio station at Glenn, which allows me to develop the expertise of that field. As my resume indicates, I spent several years in Berlin as a marketing student at Munich University and then as an intern at Berlin Media Relation Group. The training I received at these institutions was very thorough, and living in Berlin enabled me to become fluent in German. Additionally, my fluency in English, French and Mandarin Chinese in particular served me well in communicating with international media. As per your request, I have attached my resume and some writing samples to this email. I will be travelling to your city next month, if you are available. I will be pleased to meet you in person to discuss the position in detail.

I am looking forward to hearing from you.

Sincerely

Ann Heller

Unit 52

To: Jeffrey Connors <jconnors@info.de>

From: Ann Heller ann@glennbiz.com

Subject: My information / Date: January 12

It was a great pleasure meeting you at the media conference in Stockholm, Sweden on January 8. Thank you for informing me of your company's job vacancy for an international media liaison. I believe I am an ideal candidate. In my current job as public relations director of Glenn Business School in Boston, I closely work with journalists from publishers, broadcasts and online media outlets, providing news leads. In addition, I serve as a technology director of student radio station at Glenn, which allows me to develop the expertise of that field.

As my resume indicates, I spent several years in Berlin as a marketing student at Munich University and then as an intern at Berlin Media Relation Group. The training I received at these institutions was very thorough, and living in Berlin enabled me to become fluent in German. Additionally, my fluency in English, French and Mandarin Chinese in particular served me well in communicating with international media. As per your request, I have attached my resume and some writing samples to this email. I will be travelling to your city next month, if you are available. I will be pleased to meet you in person to discuss the position in detail.

I am looking forward to hearing from you.

Sincerely

Ann Heller